NOT MY CIRCUS,
NOT MY MONKEYS

NOT MY CIRCUS

NOT MY

MONKEYS

Why the Path to
Transformational
Customer Experience
Runs Through
Employee Experience

LANCE GIBBS

LIONCREST
PUBLISHING

NOT MY CIRCUS, NOT MY MONKEYS
*Why the Path to Transformational Customer
Experience Runs Through Employee Experience*

ISBN   978-1-61961-709-4 *Hardcover*
      978-1-61961-700-1 *Paperback*
      978-1-61961-701-8 *Ebook*

CONTENTS

FOREWORD

BY CLAY RICHARDSON

I have a confession to make: I've always been a business process geek. Yes, by the time I was five years old I was "that kid" who analyzed salad bars, probing for ways to improve the flow and efficiency of getting people through the line faster. My passion for business processes mushroomed over time, culminating with my position as Principal Analyst covering business process technologies and platforms at Forrester Research. But four years ago, I went through an intensive detox that destroyed my perception of the role of business processes.

My detox was kicked off by a stark conversation I had with one of my mentors, Phil Gilbert. Phil had just made the leap from running IBM's Smarter Process business unit to heading up IBM Design. At the time, Phil was a rock star in the BPM software world. So when he told me about his new "design" position, I scratched my head wondering, "Why the hell is this guy reinventing himself when he's at the top of his game?" During our conversation, Phil uttered two words that shattered my perception of business process: "design thinking." He told me that design thinking was all about putting customers at the center of any new business process or solution you're trying to build. My perception had always been that the process *was* the center of the solution and that customers were just consumers of the process.

This conversation with Phil led me on a two-year research quest, my detox, to master the art of design thinking and customer experience. I interviewed dozens of companies and learned that putting the customer at the center of your design leads to better business processes and solutions. And even more, by building empathy for the customer, companies have the potential to uncover disruptive and innovation solutions that can change the game for an entire industry. Companies like Tesla, Amazon, and Google have proven this time and time again. Just take a look at a recent earnings report from any of these companies to gain a sense of the outsized impact customer experience can have on an organization and an industry.

Today, business leaders are all focused on digital transformation. And customer experience is at the heart of delivering new digital products and services. When Lance Gibbs first shared with me his vision for this book, he made a statement that caught my attention. Lance pointed out that "digital" has become a new code word for "IT". I found that interesting because when you talk to business leaders in the IT department, they see digital as some new shiny piece of technology. But if you talk to business leaders in the marketing department, they see digital as digital marketing channels, like Twitter, Facebook, or LinkedIn. Marketing also lumps new mobile and web apps under the digital banner.

This raised the question, what exactly is "digital"? Is it about technology or is it about marketing? In *Not My Circus, Not My Monkeys*, Lance tackles this question head on. Lance argues that digital transformation is ultimately about people. Smart business leaders already know that digital transformation is driven by customer experience. But customer experience is just one dimension of the "people" equation. The blind spot that Lance zeroes in on is that the "employee experience" dimension is the most important part of driving sustainable digital transformation.

This book is intended to help business leaders build a

compelling vision and roadmap for transforming the employee experience, which is essential to delivering exceptional customer experiences. Whether you're an entrepreneur just launching a new startup or a seasoned Fortune 500 executive, this valuable insight and advice will help you unleash the potential of your most valuable resource: your employees.

—CLAY RICHARDSON
FOUNDER & CHIEF EXCELERATOR
DIGITAL FASTFORWARD
WASHINGTON, DC

INTRODUCTION

I USED TO HAVE IT ALL BACKWARDS

I got it wrong for the first ten years of my professional career. During that time, I always knew that I was getting something wrong; I just didn't know *what* it was that I was getting wrong. Then, one day, it hit me.

My moment of illumination came while I was in Seattle working on a project for a client.

The organization that I was there to assist was tasked with moving a ton of parts all over the world and had very aggressive service-level agreements in place. But the organization was consistently inconsistent in getting the parts to its customers on time. That was where my team and I came in; we were hired to assess areas for process improvement in order to better serve the client's customers. The stakes were high, and the pressure was on.

The project was brand new, and we were invited to participate in a kickoff meeting to introduce our mission and ourselves. The company had set up the meeting in a huge open area and brought in somewhere close to ninety people. My team and I were pretty taken aback because this was not traditional. Typically, kickoff meetings consist of a small number of key decision makers and an intimate presentation. But here we were *on a stage* (so to speak) with close to a hundred people looking back at us as we spoke about our approach, why we did what we did, and the roles and responsibilities involved. I looked around the room. People in the audience were visibly uncomfortable, shifting in their chairs, leaning back looking up at the ceiling, or just completely checked out.

The anxiety coming from those people in the audience was palpable; I watched the blood drain from their faces as I spoke. They looked like they were going to be sick. *What the hell was going on?*

After that big meeting, my team and I were split up and ushered into smaller breakout sessions so that we could speak more personally to smaller groups. The whole point was to start breaking things down and focusing on the real problem areas before we could start solution-ing.

I began my presentation. But then, in the middle of the session, one person just completely broke down into tears and got up and walked out of the room. We were all stunned. You could have pulled the pin out of a grenade and rolled it into the room, and we wouldn't have moved. We had never seen that kind of reaction. I suggested we take a break and tried to run the woman down. But before I could get to her, I ran into someone whom I had seen her talking to earlier in the day. I asked him if he had seen which way she went.

"No, I didn't," he said. "What happened?"

"She was pretty upset," I told him.

"Yeah, we all are," he replied.

I asked him what he meant. He told me that he and many of the other employees were upset about being asked to implement changes and do things that they were unfamiliar with because they were already under a lot of pressure to do things a certain way. They all had very high-pressure jobs as it was; it was a demanding gig, and I could tell that all of the employees felt that their jobs were on the line.

I started asking him questions like, "*What had the company done to invest in them being prepared? What kind of training had they received? How do they believe their day-to-day work will change?*"

He told me that the company hadn't invested time and resources into any kind of training for any of them. I couldn't believe that. Even before coming into the project, I figured that the company would have picked participants that had some knowledge of the methods we would be utilizing. But no, these employees were being asked to learn and implement the program on top of their regular, already stressful day jobs.

It was at this point that I realized that the company and my team were not aligned. The expectations of the executives and whoever else was spearheading the project were not the same as those of the employees and managers who would be responsible for implementing the project. Forget about not being on the same page. We weren't even remotely in the same zip code.

I thought this project couldn't get any more screwed up, but then it did. The guy I had run into in the hallway told me that the employees had never been given the agency to make decisions before, but now, they were being told that they *had* to make decisions. This meant that they were essentially being thrown to the wolves. Any wrong decision, and they would be held personally responsible. Their heads were on the line.

At that moment, I truly started to see.

I've had to deal with anxious employees on projects before, but up to that point, I had never had an emotional exchange like that in my entire career. Historically, I viewed the disposition of a client's employees as something that was just not my problem, yet this felt different and really drove home in my mind that we had a real problem on our hands. This issue was not about the company's inability to get parts to their customers. The problem—the *true problem*— was way more foundational. The problem was that the employees were suffering. That's why the business was suffering, and ultimately why the customer was suffering.

We couldn't move on with the program because it would have turned into the fucking wild bunch very quickly, given the level of despondence exhibited by the employees. Risk and cost would be unmanageable, and the odds of success would be completely against us. We had to get people all the way up and down the chain into a better place and on board if we ever stood a chance.

We tried to escalate the concerns of the employees up the

chain. But the senior managers were unwilling to hear us out. They treated us just like their employees; they gave us a pat on the head and dismissed us. They told us that if their employees were being resistant, just let senior management know, and they would "handle it."

These managers didn't understand. They heard what they wanted to hear. We weren't reporting that their employees were giving us trouble, we were reporting that their employees were lost and scared and needed help. The employees needed leadership to improve their experience, not retribution to punish them for being unhappy.

The higher-ups wanted us to implement strategy to fix their customer experience, and when we told them that we first needed to fix their employee experience, they scoffed. I realized then, as Peter Drucker has said, "Culture eats strategy for breakfast." It didn't matter what we did or how much money we pumped into our strategy. If we didn't make the employees happy, we would just be pissing up a wall.

My time on that project was the catalyst for me to start digging deeper.

I realized that companies have to care as much about the employee experience as they care about the customer experience. In fact, thcy needed to treat their employees like they treat their customers. Once they can do that, their organization will prosper, and their customers (and their bottom line) will reap the benefits.

WHERE I WAS GOING WRONG

Now, many years later, I still live in the world of "business process management," which has evolved into "digital process automation." I help companies orchestrate, automate, and instrument their core operational business processes using various technologies and techniques. My gig is extremely fulfilling; making a real difference feels good for all, especially when taking into consideration all of the challenges that we have to wade through.

Before I encountered the client mentioned above, I used to come to my clients with a playbook for improvement, ideas for implementing strategies and technology, and the experience and reputation of having done this work for years. I had my methods, my recommendations, and all of my great ideas, and—although there were differences company-to-company and business unit-to-business unit—I ran my game plan. I did this hoping that people would just *get it*. I figured they would understand, agree, eventually take the reins, and fulfill their own destinies.

But that just was not so. It sounds even more naïve as I put pen to paper!

Since that encounter with the employees up in Seattle, I have thrown away my playbook.

Trying to better areas of business for the sake of the employee, the sake of the company, and the sake of the customer is not simple—I know now that I cannot just apply a playbook; it is more complex than that. It is complex because you have to know how to pick your battles and then work with managers, employees, and executives to frame the real root cause of the problem in a singular fashion. On a good day, this shit is really hard. Add dysfunction, and now it's on like Donkey Kong!

You have to find the specific (perhaps even *narrow*) areas where you can get the biggest bang for your buck instead of trying to run programs that are too large, too wide, have too many moving parts, or necessitate the participation and agreement of too many people.

The playbook I used to stick to caused or contributed to friction and anxiety within the organizations I worked with. That was in part because my strategies just didn't fit for some companies because of the ways they invested in their employees, priorities, strategic roadmaps, or customers, or because of the way that the various functional areas of the business that processes cut across related to each other.

Even when things were relatively easy, I felt like my playbook just made things *too damn hard*. Harder than they needed to be, for sure. I approached the work with a scientific mindset (that was my background, after all), but when you add in the human factor, I promise you all that shit goes right out the window.

I was aggressively and ineffectively treating the symptoms (e.g., customer dissatisfaction or customer churn) with a one-size-fits-all methodology. I had gone into so many different companies that all of their processes were starting to look the same to me. I was losing sight of the subtleties, and taking my experiences for granted.

I learned from my time at that client in Seattle that what I needed to do was figure out how to take a very human approach to affecting a company's unique culture rather than sticking to the scientific rigor of process design principles.

THE BEGINNINGS

My background is in information technology. In the beginning of my professional IT career, I was a developer. I moved from network engineering into coding in 1995, at about the time the World Wide Web really started to pick up steam. From my vantage point as a developer, I saw a lot of change in the world. And, of course, that change resulted in a lot of fear. Fear that the world of brick-and-mortar business would be turned upside down by the World Wide Web.

And in some respects, it was. For certain companies, this change brought them to the end of their road. But for others, it was an opportunity for growth. I saw that smaller, more nimble businesses were able to take the World Wide Web by the horns and adapt their processes to their advantage. They could alter their processes faster because they were small and didn't have a lot of baggage, and there was no long chain of command to get approval from. They were early adopters, and they became successful because of it.

I saw this happening and wanted to be a part of it. So I moved from the internal IT world into the world of consulting and entrepreneurship. I began working with companies to help them establish web presences and web applications. I worked for Dell as a consultant during the company's early days on the web with Dell Online. I saw a lot of crazy-cool stuff on the e-commerce side that I had never seen before. They were doing $4 to $5 million *a day* in sales on their website!

When I saw what was happening, I decided that I wanted to get more involved with how things operated on a larger scale.

I became more interested in the processes behind business operations. This took me down the path of Lean Flow and Six Sigma, two methods of process improvement. Six Sigma was one of first methods to introduce the notion that considerations of customer experience should inform process design. I had never heard of that before. No one talked about that, I mean *nobody*. I was suddenly taking the customer into consideration more than I ever had in regards to process improvement.

It had historically been true that organizations would work to make improvements for the customer's benefit from the *"inside-out,"* believing that the total sum of improvements would make things better. And of course, that didn't—and still doesn't—hold true.

Instead, Six Sigma theories state that customer experience is an *"outside-in"* activity. And it is with that view that you should examine the people, processes, and technologies that affect customers.

Meanwhile, companies were also looking at the customer in a new light. At the time, companies started realizing the huge potential of online commerce and their strategy to capture market share was to invest heavily in front-end web design—the point at which the customer interacted online with the company. I saw this happening and knew exactly why that was their strategy. It was because front-end design is directly accretive to revenue: it is the point at which your revenue capture occurs. Because of this, companies figured that if they could invest in optimizing that experience for customers by making that purchase transaction as easy and fast as possible, they could capture more revenue.

In my opinion, this is where companies—the client I mentioned earlier included—went wrong.

I saw companies investing a lot of money in front-end technology. But they weren't investing anything in the back-end, where employees did their work. They never thought to implement useful, intuitive, or elegant interfaces or processes on the back-end because the customer never interacted with the back-end, at least not in a widely conspicuous way that was recognized by the organization. They figured that any significant investment in the backend—or their employee's experience—was just pure expense and cost.

They really just cared about the customer, and they

believed the customer was the most important variable to consider in growing profits.

Two decades later, this belief still exists. Or rather, through lack of action, this belief still *persists*.

But now things have come to a head. Companies' technological choices have caught up to them and are now biting them in the ass. Companies are still using back-end systems that should have been thrown in the trash a long time ago. However, most of these systems have just been "fixed" or "patched," as if with Band-Aids and chewing gum. It's ugly shit. It was ugly shit back then and it's even uglier shit now more than two decades later.

I could list so many examples of the ugliness, but one of my favorite examples are Interactive Voice Response systems. Interactive Voice Response, aka IVR, is the automated system that answers our calls when we call in for technical support, customer support, or to conduct over the phone payments. I'm sorry to say that, unfortunately, we all have had to use IVR. Remember the time that you had an issue with your cable provider and decided to call in to talk to a customer service agent? Remember the maze of buttons that you had to press in order to hopefully be connected with a real person? *Please press #1 for billing. Please press #2 for technical support.* That was IVR. I'll admit,

I have screamed many an expletive into the phone while interacting with an Interactive Voice Response system. I cannot believe this damned technology still exists today.

Why do things like IVR systems exist? Because they are cheap. They allow companies to hire a smaller number of people in their contact centers than necessary. The IVR systems are a poor attempt at offering self-service to customers, and always end up making customers more aggravated. The poor souls in the contact center are then burdened with angry, sometimes inane, callers. It is an absurd system where no one really wins—customers and employees both suffer. But because back-end processes like IVR may not easily be correlated to revenue using historical metrics, there is no incentive for companies to change them. So these back-end systems just sit there rotting, and employees have to sit there smelling it.

But in today's world, employees and customers alike will not stand for ugly shit like that anymore. Companies like Amazon, Grainger, Nordstrom, and, hell, even Green Mountain Coffee employ humans to answer the phones. They figured out the secret to improving their bottom line: engaging with customers directly.

I am the Founder, Executive Chairman, and former CEO of BP3 Global. At BP3, we fervently believe that every employee and every customer can have a great experience in their interactions with companies. This belief is the "why" behind the "what" and "how" of what we do. The "what" of what we do is we work to get rid of all of the ugly stuff that prevents a great experience. Finally, our "how" is we identify the root-cause problems and then work to change them through the vehicle of "people, process, and technology."

Our work gives us unique insight into the various aspects of a business, and we specialize in melding the back-end experience to the front-end experience. We pay attention to the actual "process consumers." Not just the customers, but also the people moving the ball forward from a process standpoint: the employees. Then, we ask how the processes meet *their* needs.

At BP3, we practice what we preach. We ask our employees, *"what would make your life easier, and what can we do to help you do the best you can for our customers?"*

It is such a dead, stupid simple, in-your-face obvious question, yet so few companies ask it. But we do.

The BP3 team has won a lot of awards:

- #12 Best Workplaces for Recent Grads (*Fortune* and Great Place to Work®)
- #4 Best Workplaces for Technology (*Fortune* and Great Place to Work®)
- #8 Best Small Workplaces (*Fortune* and Great Place to Work®)
- #2 Best Places to Work Medium Companies (*Austin Business Journal*)
- Fastest Growing 50 Companies in Central Texas (2012–2016) (*Austin Business Journal*)
- #1 Top Small Workplaces (*Austin Statesman*)

We know the importance of giving our employees a great experience in our quest to offer the best customer experience possible, and *we've figured out how to do it*. Although we know we can always do better! Honestly, it only took us asking ourselves—as customers, as employees, and as consumers—what was important to us. We knew that what was important to us would probably be what was important to the next person. What we found was stupid simple, and I want to share it with you.

PART ONE

THE STATE OF THE UNION

Before we launch into our findings, we must first lay the foundational knowledge of some key terms and the state of affairs in business today—more specifically, the state of customer experience, the state of employee experience, and the state of processes.

CUSTOMER EXPERIENCE

In order to understand how to improve customer experience, we must first understand what exactly customer experience is. In a word, customer experience is about feelings. It is about how a customer *feels* when he interacts with a company. If processes are efficient and employees are happy, then the customer will have a positive feeling.

The feeling that a customer has when interacting with a company is the bedrock of the customer-company relationship. If a company can make a customer feel good through his experience during four or five major interactions, then the company will earn the customer's *trust*. If the customer *trusts* the company, then he will prioritize that company over its competitors as long as that positive experience prevails. This is how a company gains a loyal following.

Customer *experience* and customer *service* are two very different things. Customer service is a discipline. The customer service representative has one job: to interact with the customer and provide a service to him. Customer service does not guarantee a great experience for a customer. Rather, customer service is the vehicle in which a great customer experience is delivered.

I believe that we, as human beings, are inclined to treat each other well. Employees want to be nice to customers, and I do believe they really try. But it's hard for them to do that if they themselves are not taken care of. If employees are taken care of and feel happy, they will be more inclined to offer great customer service time and time again. This will then translate into a great customer experience.

SOUTHWEST AIRLINES

When your career of choice is professional services, you quickly learn that you carry a bag for a living. You travel most weeks, if not *every* week. Due to my profession, I have been a frequent traveler for over twenty years. Therefore, I have seen a lot of changes in the airline industry.

At one point in my career, I had Executive Platinum status on American Airlines and Platinum status on Continental Airlines (now United) *at the same time!* But let me tell you, it was not a badge of honor.

After 9/11, there were many changes that came in to play around air travel, none of which made a frequent traveler very happy. Suddenly, lines were longer, there were fewer options and amenities offered, and the experience became exceedingly frustrating all in all. Because I spent so many hours suffering in airports, I had a lot of time to make observations. I am a process guy, so I can easily spot when process design patterns are created because they make sense or mitigate some risk versus when they are created carelessly. When I flew, I saw a lot of the latter and not much of the former. Yes, that's a judgment, and I am laying it right there: those processes were *careless.* It takes a lot to piss me off, but man, careless process design patterns really get me going.

So, after a number of years of being frustrated by the major airlines, I said, "Screw it!" I spent all the points I had banked, and trashed my loyalty cards. I decided that, for domestic flights in the US, I was going to fly Southwest Airlines. It turned out to be one of the best decisions I have ever made with regard to travel.

I had flown only a couple times on Southwest, but I

remembered one simple thing about the experience: you buy a ticket and queue up at the gate for a seat of your choosing. "Hooray," I thought. "An airline that understands queuing theory!" It was so efficient and so straightforward. Because I was hypersensitive to other airline industry players' processes, I started seeing just how different and better Southwest's were.

Most organizations, including those in the airline industry, operate like a pyramid: the first priority is their shareholders, the second is their customers, and the third is their employees. Southwest Airlines flips that pyramid on its head. Southwest cares first and foremost about their employees, then about their customers, and then about their shareholders. Southwest prioritizes their employees and customers over their stock price and short-term quarterly performance grades.

That culture trickles straight down from Southwest's leadership; namely, Colleen Barrett and founder, Herb Kelleher. Kelleher was originally an attorney who really wanted nothing to do with being CEO of Southwest. Colleen was his long-time executive assistant, and she ended up aiding him with running the company. Neither Colleen nor Herb are part of the traditional executive "club." Colleen doesn't have the elite pedigree or fancy diplomas most leadership does and Herb is known for being a sort of maverick in the business world. All they really had was a great vision, an understanding of operations and how they wanted to run the business, and an attachment to the idea of Servant Leadership.

Servant Leadership is an idea that came from Robert Greenleaf's 1977 book, *Servant Leadership: A Journey Into the Nature of Legitimate Power and Greatness.* In it, Greenleaf outlines the way in which a leader should lead: through service to his people. Once leaders can focus on that, all kinds of good things will happen because there will be trust within the employee-company relationship.

The executives at Southwest, led by Colleen and Herb, embodied this ideal; service to their employees came first. Colleen was never focused on the typical things that most leadership focuses on, such as financials, operations, or regulatory requirements. Her only focus was on Southwest's employees, day in and day out.

Colleen's service to her employees has manifested in numerous positive ways. First and foremost, the employees clearly feel appreciated and trusted because they work hard to deliver a great experience to all of their customers. Southwest has won numerous customer service awards and consistently blows their competitors out of the water in customer experience. This has led to an incredible amount of growth for the company, in all the right ways.

As Southwest grew, it never lost itself in the muck. They're still the only airline that doesn't hit customers with baggage fees. They've worked to expand their service, and are now offering flights in most places in the country. For the most part, their flights are more reasonably priced than their competitors'. Abroad, airlines trying to emulate Southwest have sprouted up.

This is all possible because Southwest's employees are happy. Dare I say, they even appear to have a good time! The service is great, it is incredibly rare to have to wait at the gate because of broken equipment, and for the most part, the airline operates on time. There are no baggage hassles and no change fees on tickets—just a simple and straightforward travel experience where the customer is not harassed. Southwest goes above and beyond, even offering proactive customer service. They are always reaching out, looking for feedback, and finding out what more they can help with.

Colleen and the other members of the executive team have created a culture where the employees feel like they can take ownership of a problem and work to solve it. Of course, it is difficult for airlines to always run smoothly.

Often, delays are out of their control due to weather or unexpected machine issues, but Southwest employees are encouraged to work through the problems to keep customers happy. They are empowered to find and offer solutions.

Employees at other companies do not have these same freedoms. As a glaring example of this, take United Airline's recent nuclear fuck up when they dragged one of their passengers out of his seat (bloodying his face in the process) because they had to make room for employees of a second United flight crew. United not only screwed over their customers, they also screwed over their own employees, who were, in fact, screwing each other over. After the passenger was dragged off, the four-member flight crew that was meant to take those now-empty seats boarded the plane and were berated by passengers. I'm sorry, but if I were one of the flight crewmembers that had just witnessed a beat down of a customer for a seat, there would be no fucking way I would get on that plane! It doesn't take a genius to figure out the little slice of hell that would be awaiting me. In the end however, because they feared what might happen to their jobs or because they were in shock, the crewmembers boarded and kept the party going. Ah, good times.

Southwest has surely overbooked flights (all airlines do) and had to move around passengers, but did the aftermath of it ever make headlines? No! That is because Southwest Airlines employees handle their shitty situations differently than United employees do. In fact, I would go as far as to say that what those employees at United did would never happen at Southwest.

But the United employees' behavior is not as uncommon as we'd all like to think. Just look at the article that came out the next day about United bumping an already seated man from his seat because "a higher priority" passenger needed it. The booted passenger was subsequently threatened with handcuffs if he didn't give up his seat. These two extraordinary events were not situational; rather, they occurred as a result of systemic issues with the culture at United.

My guess is the United employees did not feel like they could adopt these problems and own them. They didn't feel like they could make concessions or decisions about how to fix the problems. Apparently, they tried to offer United credits as the consolation prize for the bumped passengers, but not one passenger would take the credits as compensation. If it were my company, I would have had my employees offer cash—Lord knows United has the money—and an upgrade on another flight. My point is, the United employees could have offered anything! They could have gone above and beyond to make this situation work. Hell, they even could have made it work *fairly*. But instead, they didn't adopt the problem and didn't work around it. Instead, they regressed back to their Cover Your Ass mentality, and followed the policies and procedures put in place by United. You won't get out of your seat that you rightfully and legally paid for? We won't offer you cash or an upgraded seat to a new flight. No, we're going to call security and have them drag you out of the plane, bloodied and screaming.

These United employees didn't care about the customer, which tells me that that isn't a part of their culture. You can tell by the way that their CEO handled the fall out. He didn't really apologize. At least not in the first few days. Instead, he shifted blame, basically discounted his customers' feelings, and covered his ass for fear of a lawsuit. Once United's stock was down 4%, someone finally penned a more contrite response for him to issue to the public.

By contrast, Southwest is so successful because employees are cared for and respected, and that respect permeates down to the customer. There was a story that hit the news a while back about a woman who flew Southwest, and when she picked up her bag from baggage claim, she noticed that the handle had been broken. When she went to the Southwest counter at baggage claim, they offered to repair it or replace it for her. Southwest has a whole inventory of brand new travel bags at airports that they give away to customers free of charge if something happens to their bags! What is even more incredible is that this initiative was not thought of by leadership. Rather, the idea came from the employees themselves. They saw that from time to time, customers had issues with destroyed or broken bags, so they adopted the problem and worked to fix it.

The leaders of Southwest provide a trusting and compassionate environment for their employees, which allows them to continue to offer fantastic customer experience at a reasonable price. I have been flying with Southwest for seven years now, and I will never go back to another carrier.

KNOW YOUR CUSTOMER

Although companies are moving in the right direction in their quest to offer a better customer experience, most companies still don't truly understand what that means. In order to understand what it means to offer a great customer experience, they must first know their customers. However, most companies have no unified view of who their customers are.

Today, more than ever, it is important to get the view right. That is because the world is changing through the influence of a whole new generation of people who are all about extreme individualism. Many companies continue to define their customers based on older ideas of demographic delineations or other segmentation theories. But now, consumers are breaking traditional molds, and it is difficult for companies to nail down whom, exactly, these customers are, and what their journey is when interacting with an organization. But it is ever more important to understand who customers are, because these individualistic consumers demand it.

Companies have to contend with yet another hurdle when it comes to offering great customer experience: the complications that arise from the myriad of devices that customers own. Customers now live lives that revolve around their devices. For most, their phones are their center for entertainment, sports, banking, contacts, messaging, and communication. More important, their phones are available 24/7 and allow instant access to everything and anything. I bring this up because phones and other devices have transformed the expectations of most customers; they expect everything to be instantaneously available at the exact moment that they want it. Expectations are ratcheting up higher and higher all the time.

So, the question is this: Can companies start to transform

themselves in the right ways to tackle these new changes and expectations brought on by these new realities?

Companies have some choices to make. They can take on these new facts of life or deny them. They can put consumers in their place, and tell them that they should not expect much. Companies can continue to offer a slow, clunky experience, all the while sending their customers the message that they don't really give a damn about what they want, and that they just better get used to it because they have no other option.

What if I told you that, in many cases, bad customer experiences happen by design? It is true, for example, that Cost per Contact models are created to incentivize call center employees to get the customer off the phone or transferred to someone else as quickly as possible. You heard correctly. They are paid to get rid of you. In other cases, they set policies that require them to not respond to a support ticket for at least one hour. Then, if a customer calls in, they put them on hold, forcing them to listen to the voice that "entertains" them while they're on hold—the voice that tells them about how awesome the company's premium support offering is and reminds them to ask about it. It is all by design.

I'm not the brightest guy in the room, but it is clear to me that companies are fucking with customers at their own peril. The days of customers being held captive are over.

In "Digital Disconnect in Customer Engagement," a recent report published by Accenture, researchers polled 24,489 customers in thirty-three countries and eleven different industries, and found that 52% of customers have switched providers of goods and services because of poor customer service. The estimated cost in the US alone of customers switching due to poor service is $1.6 trillion. The report also found that 83% of US consumers prefer dealing with human beings to digital channels.

So, the only other path is through the second option: Companies have to get very serious and very self-reflective. They have to sit down, shut up, and listen. Then, they have to put in place a game plan to determine what investments to make in order to become players in this new climate.

Each and every company is going to have their own day of reckoning in some form or fashion. They can do a lot of things in the meantime to place Band-Aids and chewing gum over their wounds, but the clock is ticking.

One of my favorite examples of a company that has refused to up their game to offer good customer experience is Comcast.

Ed Oswald writes for *The CheatSheet* and chronicles companies with horrific customer service. About Comcast, he writes:

"No call center horror stories are more frequent than those involving Comcast. The cable provider has already won the title of one of the most hated companies in America, and a lot of that has to do with how it treats its customers. The company was caught red-handed in 2014 with its heavy-handed retention tactics when a phone operator essentially interrogated journalist Ryan Block, who recorded the call. It's also allegedly managed to get a former customer fired, and even told a widow that her dead husband needed to cancel service. Really.

Comcast claims that it's working on improving customer service, telling the *New York Post* that it believes recent investments in improving the call center experience are helping it to stem the loss of subscribers to online streaming services. We'll see: A thread on Reddit for shoddy Comcast experiences still seems way too active."

Perhaps not terribly surprising is that the five worst-rated companies for customer experience are all cable providers and telecommunication companies. These companies have enjoyed a monopoly in the markets where they operate due to the competition restrictions in place. Many years ago, these companies sold the idea that since they have to spend a lot of capital to build infrastructure, they deserve to have a period where they don't have to worry about competition. Now, they find themselves in a real pickle: They are beginning to be disrupted, and their brand has taken more damage than a Ford Pinto at a demolition derby.

There are some companies, however, that do a great job of offering white-glove service all the way through the customer lifecycle—even after the close of the sale. Nordstrom is a great example of this and a great counterexample to a company like Comcast. Nordstrom's products are not cheap; you pay for what you get. But there is no bait and switch. You are taken care of if something goes wrong. For example, Nordstrom has a 24/7 customer service line, where every call must be answered by the second ring. You can consistently find Nordstrom employees going above and beyond. Often times, there is no line at any register. This is part of the basic customer experience that Nordstrom offers.

Another great example of a company that goes beyond is a Dutch company called Jeans Online. They offer a service where you can go online, pick out the clothes you want, and then a courier will bring your jeans right to your door so that you can try them on and keep what you want. If you don't like anything, you just hand them back to the courier, and they're gone!

There is a lot of enabling technology out there that companies could be using to add that white-glove element to their customer experience without breaking the bank. I think it is especially important for relationship-based companies to always be searching for new technologies that could improve their customer experience. Relationship-based companies would really benefit from technology that fosters a white glove type feel for customer service.

The use of video is a great example of a technology with untapped potential. I can FaceTime with anyone I want, but I can't use FaceTime with my bank, for instance, which holds every asset I own. It would be great to get to use video as an option with a customer service rep when I feel like I need a face-to-face interaction. This would benefit both the bank and me because the bank could offer great service while building a deeper relationship. Then, when it came time for renewals or expansions, the trust would already be there.

The possibilities of video conferencing are endless! I'm thinking it could be applicable across many different industries. I could video in to get help getting a document completed, an appliance fixed, or when my tire blows out.

Online notaries who conduct business via video conference are already a reality in the state of Virginia; it won't be long before this is supported in more states.

Unfortunately, many relationship-based companies are not getting the picture that they have access to some powerful tools and techniques that could improve their customer experience by optimizing the human-to-human and human-to-system interactions. Transactional companies (companies that offer goods or services on a one-time basis) are even less willing or able to investigate the potential of available tools and strategies that could improve their customers' experiences.

CUSTOMER LOYALTY IS DEADER THAN FRIED CHICKEN

It is more important than ever for companies to assess their customer experience offerings because if they don't, they will find themselves losing customers *fast*.

This is because today, by and large, customer loyalty is dead. It's deader than fried chicken. It just simply does not exist like it used to. Customers have access to more choices and information than ever before. This is mostly due to the supremacy of the Internet; if we want to hire a new plumber, we can look up a dozen on Angie's List. If we want to buy a new TV, we don't read Sony or Samsung advertisements, we look at reviews and reach out for opinions via our social networks. We don't have to trust the words of companies; we can go to hundreds of different review sites to find the truth. Customers are no longer tied to brands. Trust is hard to maintain and establish. Loyalty is fleeting.

Now more than ever, companies must hold on to their customers. And a no-brainer way to do this is through offering a great customer experience.

Many companies have sprung up that take advantage of other companies that fear fickle and flighty customers. These companies promise new ways and approaches to cementing customer loyalty by optimizing the customer experience in order to stand out from competitors. However, a lot of these promises are just *noise*.

I see a lot of companies desperately trying to retain customer loyalty and falling prey to the noise. They end up purchasing services from various providers with lofty promises claiming they have found a new, silver bullet way to gather customer insights and change the business overnight! There seem to be countless startups out there chasing this wave and espousing new ways to achieve customer success by digital transformation. There are a lot of big buzzwords, but not a lot of efficacy.

I've also seen companies carelessly throwing their money into one or many apps. They wrongly believe that an app is at most a quick fix to all of their customer experience problems, and at least another way to compete. Companies end up pissing away a lot of money on social media apps or mobile apps that they build under the assumption that they are improving customer experience. But most of the time, those mobile apps don't really help anything.

Companies can't ensure a good customer experience—much less enduring customer trust and loyalty—by paying for a new mobile app. An app is a sweet gift, for sure, but once a customer gets past the fancy UX-design packaging, they'll find that their access to help has not actually improved. I've seen companies brag about having twelve or fourteen apps for their customers, like it's some sort of badge of honor. But what it is is lipstick on a pig.

I don't know of any company that is really that good at measuring and tracking internal success rates of digital transformation programs. It is a tough thing for most companies, as they usually get hung up in the budgeting and ROI portion of the program. It is also difficult to quantify the impact of something that is as esoteric as "experience." Companies need to first determine how to go about tracking and measuring success rates. They need to determine what measures they want to track and then verify that they are effective and viable. Then, companies need to gather an effective sample size that is meaningful. For many businesses that have longer-term sales cycles, higher priced buys, bigger buy decisions, and/ or are relationship-based businesses, these metrics can take a long time to figure out.

Sometimes, companies think they know how to accurately measure and track success rates. But nine times out of ten, they're chasing the wrong metrics. Then, they wonder why their digital transformation programs are unsuccessful. The 15% or so of companies that claim that their digital transformation initiatives *were* successful are in a small field. Most do not successfully solve their problems because they did not really know what their problems were in the first place!

In short, offering great customer experience has a hell of a lot less to do with the technology, and a lot more to do with people. If you are focusing on the noise of technology, you won't be able to hear the noise that your customers are making.

How can companies go about massively improving their customer experience? Certainly not through any magical technological feat. Rather, companies can achieve this by improving the experience of their greatest asset— their employees.

EMPLOYEE EXPERIENCE

There is a no doubt, no bullshit, positive correlation among the employee experience, the customer experience, and the performance of the business. For example, the Temkin Group found a correlation between efforts in employee engagement and success in customer experience. In its 2016 Employee Engagement Benchmark Study, the firm revealed that companies that excel at customer experience have "1.5 times as many engaged employees as do customer experience laggards." In the December 2016 *Harvard Business Review* article, "Design Your Employee Experience as Thoughtfully as You Design Your Customer Experience," Denise Lee Yohn cited a Gallup study that said that while a staggering 87% of employees worldwide are not engaged, companies with highly engaged workforces outperform their peers by 147% in earnings per share. Recently, more and more of these studies have been making their way into the mainstream.

Employee experience highly correlates to customer experience. *Period.*

We can examine this through our Southwest Airlines case. The employees who work at Southwest Airlines are happy. It didn't take my sub-par investigative skills to figure this out—you can just tell. Southwest's priorities are in this order: employees, customers, shareholders.

The employees who work at Southwest have a difficult job to do. They work in travel, after all. They work face-to-face with customers in a very fast-paced environment that demands a lot of patience and understanding. They have to care for travelers, serve them and clean up after them. They must work together and work together *well.*

Because of this, one can understand how easy it would be for the Southwest employees to fall victim to drama and internal squabbles. But they don't. Southwest's leadership believes in proactive customer service, starting with the employees. These employees have a real team spirit. The company fosters strong relationships both inside and outside of work, and because of this, there is a great degree of trust among teams and their managers. This nurtures a culture where the employees see themselves as crucial pieces of the value chain. Southwest truly invests in their employees and, therefore, they feel important. Because of this, they feel incentivized to deliver a great customer experience.

They're encouraged to do just about anything that could create a better experience for the customer. They have a lot of freedom and autonomy to do what they think is best, and Southwest is open to hearing their ideas. The managers ask the employees how they are doing, talk about feedback from customers, discuss complaints, and spitball ways to make things better.

If you look at the same kind of situation in the call centers or contact centers where I've worked over the years, employees and leadership don't typically tend to have conversations like this. They have their staff meetings and they talk about major issues, or review some policy, or discuss policy changes. But these sessions always turn into more of a monologue by the manager rather than a dialogue in which everyone is involved.

This doesn't foster the same camaraderie and trust as seen at Southwest. Dialogues allow managers and leadership to demonstrate a certain level of vulnerability. They are forced to admit their mistakes or to say, "I got it wrong." Admissions such as these create an environment where real discussion about whether policies and procedures are relevant and/or are working is allowed.

In an environment where questioning and admissions of guilt are not allowed, people just kind of have to throw their hands up; they pass the buck, and nothing gets changed. They say things such as, "well, that's not really our call," or "that's not our decision, we have to go up the chain to ask permission." This sends the message that change is not okay. It affects employee motivation in the end, because people feel that they can't change outdated or irrelevant policies. This, by the way, is by design; there is a motivational bias for change not to occur. No worker wants to fight the status quo and possibly lose his job.

Throughout my many years of consulting, many employees have opened up to me—no holds barred—about the good and the bad of the companies that they work at. They have been willing to open up because they have seen me as a safe avenue—not a person to vent to, but rather an outlet to whom they can communicate honestly about what they need and what they want to change. It is dangerous for them to speak candidly like this to their higher-ups, because they might be viewed as bucking the system or thinking that they are smarter and have grander ideas than their bosses. They're stuck between a rock and a hard place.

Change can't come only when Rome is burning. It's too late to do anything if things are on fire, revenue is slipping, or customer attrition is high. Ironically, if things are not on fire, and the company is chugging along, no one will want to speak out to change things. When no one speaks out, employees become demoralized and demotivated. They feel as though they don't matter.

Southwest succeeds in its customer experience goals because it truly invests in the success and experience of its employees. It fosters a culture where employees understand where they fit into the value chain and are incentivized to deliver a great customer experience.

I am a frequent Southwest customer, and I reap the benefits of a great culture. My great experience is highly correlated to the employees' great experience

THE TRUTH ABOUT COMPANIES AND THEIR EMPLOYEES

Unfortunately, very few companies are as incredible as Southwest is at offering an exceptional employee experience.

Why is this so? In order to explain, I have to paint an

honest—but depressingly unflattering—picture of how companies think about and treat their employees.

First and foremost, **companies don't truly see the inherent value in their employees or how to maximize their talent.** To many companies, employees are just another asset—just the same as computers or software. Rarely does any money get put into protecting and bettering those assets. I believe one reason for this is that companies are unable to determine a direct return on investment in their employees and all the various roles they represent. Companies don't seem to understand that a direct investment in their employees positively affects the employees' relationship with customers and thus positively affects the bottom line. In the Southwest Airlines example, the employees are assigned value, and thus, they are happy. This happiness translates to the customer when they interact with them. If I have an interaction with an employee who is clearly unhappy to be at work, I will not be able to enjoy myself and will leave with a bad feeling about that company.

There are some companies that claim they are working to understand the return on investment in their employees and have very robust programs underway. These companies are typically on the business-to-consumer side. Some startups kind of get it, but others are failing miserably.

Uber claims to be working hard to understand how to deliver a great employee experience, yet many employees work tremendous hours and don't feel appreciated. Just look at the executive turnover at Uber recently, and what the folks departing have said publicly. Even when companies claim to be trailblazers, many are still shitshows behind the scenes.

There are companies that can do it, though! I met with David Skomo, SVP and Chief Pharmacy Officer at a Fortune 100 healthcare company, and asked him about how his organization is able to offer a great employee experience. It was clear to me that, first and foremost, the company actually cares about and understands the inherent value of their employees. David says that, "Without a good employee experience, you're dead in the water, because if your employees aren't happy to come to work every day and they're not happy with where the organization is heading, that's gonna come through very loudly due to the customers that we interface with on a daily basis."

The company measures their employee satisfaction and drives employee engagement through their Vital Signs Survey. It is an annual survey where the organization asks its employees what they would like them to invest in in terms of the employee experience. The company takes the results of this survey very seriously, which helps employees understand that management sees the value in them.

Companies are also **bad at empowering their employees.** A good customer experience begins and ends with the people who are administering it—the employees who are on the front lines dealing with customers face-to-face. For this reason, it is crucial that those employees feel that they have agency to make decisions and get answers for customers. However, many companies have kept employees from feeling as though they have the power to do so. The way these companies are organized does not promote an employee reaching out across functional areas to seek help. Employees do not feel safe to reach out because they are concerned about how their supervisors and managers will perceive it. Most of the time, deeply entrenched bureaucracy and irrelevant policy and procedures create obstacles for the correct administration of customer service. The employees at Southwest, however, are given the power to make their own customer service decisions. Companies need to understand the critical importance of letting some power into the hands of their staff.

Companies **treat their employees like machines** instead of human beings. Companies wrongly feel like they can get away with this because they administer paychecks. They think that they have the upper hand in the relationship and therefore don't see the need to care. Employers take their employees for granted in a way they don't take their customers: They foolishly assume employees are within their control, not the uncontrolled variable that they really are.

Employees are not just employees. They are humans, and they are also consumers. They go to the doctor, they buy insurance, they have cable TV and a mobile phone, they go out to eat and to the movies, they fly on planes, and they go to school. They're consumers just like anyone else. They have their biases, their likes and dislikes, and their opinions and feelings.

When hiring, companies do all that they can to filter out those individuals that might challenge the fact that they are treated like machines. When hiring, companies look at three big things: personality, adaptability, and capability. When assessing personality, they ask themselves whether the employee will get along with coworkers. When assessing capability, they ask if the candidate can learn or already has the skills to do a job. When they assess adaptability, they look to see if the potential employee is there to buck the system. They want to know if the candidate will follow procedure and policy without question.

That's it. That's how companies hire. *Three criteria.* When you hear that an employee wasn't hired because he or she wasn't a "culture fit," this is code for "there is a problem with the personality or adaptability of that individual." That individual is not a monkey or a machine, and therefore he is a risk to the company.

Companies also **don't give employees the proper tooling** to do a good job. Oftentimes, employees have to work with technology, equipment, and or processes that are antiquated. Not only does this prevent employees from doing their jobs efficiently and effectively, but it is also demoralizing. It sucks to be living in a world where you can get anything through your smartphone, but when you step into work, you have to step back twenty years in time. Unfortunately, in an age where people are empowered to tailor their lives around their own social, emotional, and functional needs, when they step into a workplace that is backwards, this leads to a strange cognitive dissonance.

Every day, employees utilize technology such as mobile apps to accomplish exactly what they need. Why can't they feel the same satisfaction with the processes that they perform at work? Companies could do right by their employees by offering contemporary tooling that mimics the tools they use in their normal lives. If more companies would integrate their processes and systems with the wide range of devices in use, employees could live a more mobile work-life. This could allow them the flexibility to work where and when they need to without having to be tethered to their desktops.

Slack is a great example of a system that allows employees the ability to interact with their company in the same way as they interact with their friends and family. Slack eliminates the need for emailing everything. Instead, you can create what is called a "channel," where you can invite anyone (and any number of people) to join in an instant and collaborative communication environment that mimics social networks.

Facebook is taking a page out of Slack's book and launching "Facebook at Work," AKA "Workplace," which is effectively an internal Facebook for enterprises. This may be a great way for companies to bring a Facebook-like atmosphere to their corporate communications.

Employees are themselves, of course, savvy consumers of products and services; in particular, they use their smartphones to execute all kinds of specific outcomes. But when employees complain or make suggestions for improvement, higher-ups do not want to hear it. Modernization means money, and, as discussed above, employers do not understand the ROI of improving the lives of their employees.

Employees are told to shut up and deal with ancient

technology. But when employees are forced to work with outdated systems, they can't do the best possible job for customers. For instance, good customer experience necessitates complete and accurate information. A customer service representative—or whoever is at the front lines of a company talking with customers—should have all of a customer's information right in front of them in *one* virtual repository. That information should be complete. It should point to a unified consensus of who that person is as a customer. This information should include a basic profile that outlines buying history, the customer's journey, and some of the defining characteristics of the account.

I want to highlight what I said before: All of the customer's information should be in *one virtual* repository. This way, representatives won't have to spend time toggling from one console to the next. However, more often than not in these antiquated systems, there are packets and pieces of data in various applications all over the organization. This prohibits employees from properly doing their jobs. Companies have been on a tear for a while now, trying to unify that customer entity into a single source, but they are far from this reality. They're still working through twenty-year modernization programs that should have ended a long time ago. Again, instead of bandaging and patching these systems, they are better off dumping them and starting from scratch if they still find themselves so many years into remediation without an end in sight.

But they won't do this because **companies are afraid of change**. Within companies, there is always a lot of lip service about how change is one of their top priorities. But when they say they like change, what they're really saying is that change is great...as long as it happens to somebody else. Change is intrinsically very difficult. The human brain avoids change as a form of self-preservation. Nonetheless, if at its core, an organization doesn't have the facilities, the infrastructure, or the training, change is nearly impossible to accomplish. Companies are risk-averse, and change is very risky, so they just don't deal with it.

But sometimes companies are forced to change, and when this happens, many are really terrible at helping their employees deal with it. Change management is not taken nearly as seriously as it needs to be. It is almost as if there are no good processes or procedures for change management because companies want to pretend it doesn't need to happen.

Some companies have a whole group of folks within HR called "change managers," who are supposed to go around helping people get comfortable with whatever change is coming. The fact of the matter is, in the entirety of my career, I have yet to come across even one company that does even a remotely "okay" job with this department. Honestly, I'd even go as far as to say companies are horrible at it.

It is very common to find that there is only one person in a company's whole "change management" department. Granted, the person probably has a Ph.D. in organizational psychology or change management, or perhaps an MBA, but all too often, they're a one-man show in an organization of 50,000 people. Adding to this, it is not shocking to find the only reason that that one person was employed in the first place was that there was a big blow-up at some point prior. The company was probably then forced by their lawyers to implement a "team" in order to legally cover their asses. So the company complied, and cobbled together a quick fix.

I don't mean to come off as sounding so cynical about all of this. But I do want to be honest: Large company customer and employee experience is in really bad shape. On a scale of 1 to 10, employee and customer experience is a 3.

There is a great scene in the original Willy Wonka movie where one of the children, Violet, eats a piece of gum that she was told not to eat. Willy Wonka sits in the background of the scene, muttering "No, stop, don't." You can feel the futility of the situation, because even as Violet turned blue and started to blow up, she would not stop chewing the gum. It was fruitless for him to attempt to mediate the situation, so he didn't. This type of apathy is what I see all too often in the business world.

It is not as though Willy Wonka or the folks in the business world have bad intentions; they are not trying to be malicious or vindictive. But some of the biggest problems I've come across arise from those people who are only there to punch a time clock or climb a ladder. This is a common disposition among those in my generation.

But the problem is that companies have *no idea* what the hell to do with this new generation that doesn't just want to just punch a time clock. When these young people realize that companies don't know how to handle them, they become miserable and start to job-hop. They represent a whole new challenge!

When an employee does show "loyalty" and stays and performs, they may be rewarded with a promotion, most likely to a middle-management gig. But the fact that someone is a damn good individual contributor does not mean he will make a good manager. This is because in order to be a good manager, he or she ideally should be a good leader. They can get by managing without leadership skills by working their employees with spreadsheets and bottom lines, but no one truly wins in that scenario. True leadership comes from someone who is the center of gravity for innovation, change, and betterment; people are drawn to them.

Unfortunately, employees also have to deal with **a crisis in leadership**. Crisis in leadership is a very real, very big problem today, and the negative effects are unprecedented. I could write a whole other book about it! Employees have no support or guidance from the top because the management infrastructure is weak. Frankly, companies have engineered leadership out of their organizations by design. They just don't want anyone with bright ideas around. They want standardization, homogenization, and people who will fall in line.

My team and I were working on a large project at a large financial services company and suggested to an executive that we move a couple of natural leaders from one particular group into leadership roles. We needed help from leadership to affect change. The executive told me that they "had none of those" and that they didn't hire people "like that." Instead, he said, they hired "monkeys" because monkeys do exactly what is asked of them without question.

Companies aren't built for leadership at scale because they're engineered against risk and change. If you watch people who are really effective at leading (either by nature or by nurture), they won't stay around an organization for long. They'll go to smaller companies or start their own businesses. They move on and move out.

This crisis in leadership leads me to my second-to-last point: **Without leaders, there is no permission to innovate.** When I see a mandate to innovate within a corporation, the mandate is either given to someone at the top, or it is given to a small group within the corporation that is tasked with improving processes or fostering fresh ideas for a company the size of Dell or IBM. These are usually teams of six to twenty-four people who are tasked with changing processes or defining new products or services for tens or hundreds of thousands of people! How much political capital could a team of six possibly hold in a company the size of IBM? And even if they did have a respectable amount of political capital, how much political capital would they be willing to burn to push their findings and offer solutions to create change if the employees of an organization weren't a large part of formulating the idea?

Lastly, today's environment **mandates conformity.** But absolute conformity is just not good. In October 2016,

Francesca Gino published a report in the *Harvard Business Review* titled "Let Your Workers Rebel." In it, Gino argues that companies need to start understanding just how destructive the widespread issue of conformity is in the workplace. She says that "those who felt they could express their authentic selves at work were, on average, 16% more engaged and more committed to their organizations than those who felt they had to hide their authentic selves." She chronicles the efforts of an owner of a fast food joint and what happened to his company after he got rid of a conformity-driven workplace. He found "customer satisfaction scores of 98% and health inspection scores above 97%. Turnover at the assistant manager level [was] under 2%. In the three decades since they got rid of the conformity-driven workplace, the fast food joint has lost only seven general managers—two of them to retirement. Annual turnover on the front lines is about 34%—half the industry average."

The impulse toward conformity in the workplace creates lots of inauthentic situations, lowers people's motivations and production, and lowers the bar for innovation.

This leads to the bad kind of nonconformity: destructive nonconformity. Destructive nonconformity leads to trouble. The recent Wells Fargo scandal is a good representation of destructive nonconformity. Their salespeople were under extreme pressure to make crazy quotas and told to do whatever it took to hit their numbers. So they did. They ended up veering off the path of morality, and their higher-ups turned a blind eye. In the end, 5,300 people lost their jobs because of it.

Wells Fargo had destructive nonconformity. What a well-functioning company needs is what is called constructive nonconformity. An environment with constructive nonconformity mandates that employees challenge the status quo bias. The company accepts those challenges and promotes criticism and critique. Companies that have constructive nonconformity allow—and even urge—employees to think outside of the box. They allow their employees to buck the system...in the quest for betterment. Things end up happening, obstacles end up coming down, and it is all done without losing sight of what is right.

Millennials are anti-authoritarian. They don't dig conformity and are more fearless about being nonconforming than their predecessors ever were. As Millennials pour into the workplace, companies need to figure out very quickly how to introduce an atmosphere of constructive nonconformity to support the businesses of today and tomorrow.

HOW TO CHANGE FOR THE BETTER

How can companies overcome their history of mistreating their employees and change for the better? How can they go about giving their employees an experience that echoes the way that they live in the modern world?

The first thing that companies have to figure out is where to start. If you are a company with 250,000 employees, how do you even begin to change things? It's almost like a physics problem: The bigger the mass of the object, the more energy it takes to move it.

In my experience, the answer lies in adopting the idea of constructive nonconformity. Once a company recognizes that this is what it is missing, it is just a matter of having the fortitude to change it. By "it" I mean processes, such as how people collaborate, how the organizational design evolves to make the best work happen, the ways in which you gain visibility into where the work is, as well as engaging employees and allowing them to feel safe in their feedback, etc. This is what it takes: deep engagement. We're not putting a man on the moon or splitting molecules with a butter knife. This is simple, hometown, apple pie kind of stuff. Once we can change engagement for the better, we can change employees' experiences for the better, and ultimately, we can change customer experience for the better.

David Skomo said that, "If we don't offer a really good employee experience, then we might as well hang it up. Because employee experience is probably the number one contributing factor to a good customer experience."

PROCESSES

THE WORK PROCESSES OF YESTERDAY, TODAY, AND TOMORROW

Southwest Airlines figured out how to design their processes for the benefit of everyone. Their fantastic employee experience and unbeatable customer experience reflects it. But what exactly about their processes makes the company run so damned well? I did some more investigation into the behind the scenes at Southwest in order to find out.

What I found was that Southwest had established well-thought-out processes. The leadership had implemented a very robust employee engagement model. The staff was provided with effective tooling. The staff also had access to a large support staff so that if someone was out for the day, they could fill the gap easily. All of these things and more served to equip Southwest employees with the necessary resources to be successful and happy in their jobs, and to provide customers with a fantastic experience.

The Southwest Airlines case illustrates just how important it is to provide employees with quality interfaces and tooling in the work that they perform. Employee experience cascades into customer experience; the better the needs of the employees are met, the better their ability will be to create a great outcome for the customer.

FOCUSING ON THE WRONG THINGS

The problem is, though, that companies fall short in designing and implementing processes for their employees. Why is that? In order to understand why companies fall short in designing and implementing processes, we must first understand processes in the larger scheme of the corporate climate.

The traditional methods of implementing organizational design are based on Frederick Winslow Taylor's idea of scientific management. In all honesty, his theories are antiquated and have no place in today's new corporate climate for two reasons: today's increasingly decentralized corporate models and a highly individualized workforce.

Taylor's theories are no longer applicable because companies in his time were structured very differently than they are now. In Taylor's time, companies were centralized. Companies operated out of one building, in one city. Companies were vertically integrated, meaning that all the work that a company needed to accomplish was done in-house. But this is just not how things work now. Companies have become decentralized; they operate across the globe, and outsourcing work has become the norm.

Technology is the reason why this decentralized corporate model exists. Technology allows teams and individuals to work together from all over the world. An employee can live in Los Angeles and work for a boss who operates out of Chicago.

Not only are employees within the corporation farther away from each other than ever before, but employees are also farther away from the customer than ever before. Customers in Seattle are talking to customer service representatives in call centers in India, the US, or Nepal.

Automation has also been a factor in decentralization, and it will continue to be so. Eventually, every single function that can be automated will be automated. I see automation happening more broadly in processes. One vehicle in the automation of processes is called robotic process automation, or RPA. In RPA, little software robots that run on your machine can execute far more efficiently than any person can. Basically, the robots can navigate multiple applications to complete a job instead of an employee having to toggle endlessly through a customer relationship management (CRM) application, mainframe application, supply chain application, and so on. There are even some software robots out there that can basically execute a very complex script from start to finish!

To the point: The centralized corporate empire has disintegrated. In effect, it's the same thing that happened to computing. We started out with giant, centralized mainframe computers that became decentralized when we all got personal desktops. Now, the computing environment has become even more decentralized because we all have mobile computing devices. This makes the computing world highly, highly, highly decentralized.

Taylor's organizational design school of thought has also become outdated because it is predicated heavily on the principle of enforced employee cooperation.

Yes, *enforced cooperation*. That really was his term for it.

It sounds authoritarian, right? That's because it is. Enforced cooperation inherently necessitates the complete control of the employee. There was no open discussion among managers and employees about how things should work or how they should change. Processes and procedures were dictated by the few for the many.

Employees were deterred from acting or speaking out because it was just too politically expensive for them to do so. Employees were terrified of being deemed "subversive," "nonconformist," or "difficult," and being fired because of it.

But today's workforce is almost unimaginable by those historical models. Everyone is very independent, very self-reliant, and pretty much unfettered in comparison.

Warehousing employees and departments together to enforce cooperation is now expensive and wasteful. Productivity is slowed, and the bottom line is affected.

I believe that corporations are on track to become even more decentralized than they already are. In fact, one school of thought that I happen to agree with is that the corporate model that exists today will soon become extinct. Instead, "corporations" will be comprised of a small number of core or key individuals who are surrounded by a constellation of affiliated network specialists. The people who exist on the periphery will perform very specific, specialized tasks.

PROCESSES ARE NOT CENTRALIZED

We must accept this new reality and prepare ourselves to work in organizations that have been distributed to the furthest extent through automation and technology, and are manned by workers who are highly individualized.

In order to prepare, we must acknowledge that the process definitions that we've had in place based on Taylor's school of thought are applicable only to the traditional, centralized corporate structure. Because the corporate world is continuing to become more and more decentralized, it is imperative that we update processes to match.

The Problem with Silos

The primary obstacle to implementing modern processes is that companies are comprised of many functional units that have become siloed. When a functional unit becomes siloed, it means each department only sees and understands the small part of the work that they are tasked with doing. For example, the sales department might only understand the sales portion of the customer lifecycle, but the salespeople have no idea what account managers do. Silos prevent employees from seeing how work flows through processes. Thus, they are unable to understand or even see how and where processes break down or become inefficient.

A recent ordeal that I had with Farmer's Insurance reflects the problem with siloed departments within corporations. I spent about forty-five minutes on a phone with a Farmer's customer service agent named Sarah because of an issue that I was having with my account. Sarah told me many times that she couldn't accomplish a pretty simply task for me. Instead of working to figure out whom I should talk to instead, the best she could do was give me another 800 number that would deliver me into a different part of the company for technical support. Sarah was extremely unhelpful, but in effect, that was all she could really do for me. The individual departments within Farmer's are so siloed that Sarah could only help me if my problem could be solved by the limited work that she is allowed to perform. I went from being on the phone with Sarah, who was trying to get a copy of my auto insurance ID card, to a call center in India for technical support, and then all the way back to my agent because he needed to submit a request to the IT group on his end in order to grant me access to my auto insurance ID card via their website. But Sarah didn't know the process; all she could do was hand me off to technical support, who also couldn't help. Then, I had to take the issue back to my agent. It took a whole week to grant me access to my ID cards online.

Once upon a time, Sarah might have been able to stand up from her desk, walk across the room to Brian in tech support, and ask him to help with my problem. But that was the centralized corporation of yesteryear. Now, companies are so decentralized that this image is laughable. At Farmer's Insurance, tech support is halfway across the globe.

Typically, in today's world, I see companies with employees who are blind as bats when it comes to where and how work flows before and after it hits their desks. A loan processor doesn't really know what happens to that loan after it leaves her hands. All she cares about is what is happening to the loan when it is directly in front of her. She wants to make sure that she is hitting her metrics and executing the required service-level agreements. She cares a lot about her cycle time, or how long it takes her to process the loan, because that is seen as a major factor in giving a great customer experience.

Because employees are so blind as to what and where their work is along the process pipeline, Sarah has no idea where to direct my problem. She might send me over to Department X or Group Y. Perhaps she might put a little flag on my incident that designates it as "high priority," but what ends up happening then? What happens is that Department X starts getting high priority flags on 90% of the incidents that they get!

Silos not only prevent employees from interacting with

other employees in different departments, but they also prevent employees from interacting with the actual customer. Many employees never even touch a customer. For example, the IT department may only ever interact with internal employees. Therefore, the people in IT have no idea what the actual customer looks like. Therefore, they feel removed from the mission of their fellow employees in benefiting the outside customer.

Employees lack vision into where the work is because of siloed structures. This is a massive problem. Silos prevent employees from understanding where the weak points and bottlenecks in processes are. For this reason, companies are going to need to get a hell of a lot better at allowing their employees insight into the processes involved in working with customers.

More and more, I see companies trying to fix their processes. However, they aren't going about it anywhere near as effectively as they could be. They aren't working to bridge their siloed departments so that everyone can see and understand processes. Rather, they are going about it by throwing large amounts of money into technologies that promise to mend holes.

That strategy is complete crap because critical business processes cut across silos.

Digital Strategies Are Misguided

I see many companies being seduced into spending big money on the newest technologies coming out of Silicon Valley—and everywhere else for that matter—that promise to immediately fix all inadequate processes, both on the front-end at the customer level and the back-end at the employee level. I've seen so many companies buy Product X or partner with Company Y because they promise that their solution will be a quick fix to all of the company's problems.

Let me say it again: That promise is crap.

Many companies out there think that building out a fancy mobile app or a sleek microsite will improve customer service. Although customers might like the look of a fancy app, the "improvement" is isolated to the front-end—to the tip of the spear, where the customer connects with the business. The customer's actual experience is not improved because processes on the back-end are still broken. A great looking website doesn't help employees help the customer any better than an old looking one does.

Most banks have mobile banking apps. Some of their apps might look nice and feel nice, but what do they look like under the hood? Are they actually delivering the value that was implied? What happens, for instance, if I see a transaction that I don't recognize? There should be a button next to that transaction that I can click that immediately brings me into a conversation with a customer service representative. That rep should have all of my account information on his console and be able to confirm that he sees why I'm calling him. All he needs to do is confirm with me that I am calling about that particular transaction, and once he gets my confirmation, he hangs up and files a dispute. If he needs the information to go to another department, he won't have to transfer me; he could take down all of the information and send the incident to the other department himself.

Minutes later, I should get a notification on my mobile app that says, "Jim Doe in fraud investigation has received your incident, his email is jim@bank.com, and his direct phone number is 800-555-5555, ext. 222. Give him 24 hours to look into and process your incident, and he will contact you."

That is how it should work. But that is certainly not how it works.

There are some CRM applications out there today that are okay, but they aren't really deserving of their title because they do not truly "manage" a customer's expectation. In truth, they are just systems that log and audit customer interactions in addition to providing some information into that customer's history. They don't really help employees understand their customers so they can proactively address their needs.

Trello is a cool application for the management of projects. But I think there is room for something even more comprehensive.

For example, the home remodeling industry could use a badass app to improve its grossly inefficient processes. While there exist some newer project management applications for construction management, they fall short from an end-customer's perspective. Instead of an app with only a task management functionality, there should be an application where the electrician, plumber, framer, designer, and anyone else involved with the process could have a profile on the app that not only tracks their job progression but also allows for collaboration in real time. At any given time, a homeowner could see what their contractors were doing, a timeline of the process pipeline, product pricing catalog, issue approvals to change requests right then and there via digital signature, and address issues such as late shipments and missed inspections. There could be a messaging system where the homeowners and various project teams could have conversations and address questions without having to go through the contractor as the middleman, who sometimes becomes more of a bottleneck than a facilitator. This wouldn't require excluding the general contractor, of course, but rather provide visibility for all.

This app isn't just about digitizing work and getting rid of middlemen and unnecessary paper. It is also about including and integrating all relevant parties—whether they're individuals, entire departments, or third parties—who would normally be siloed into one place where they can all understand what is happening in the home-building process.

This app could really benefit how homes are remodeled from the customer's perspective and reduce rework for the providers. But the app has implications across other industries as well. Currently, within businesses, process information and statuses are hidden within departments on spreadsheets and in emails. The data and information is passed from team to team on a spreadsheet or housed in a document management system. However, there is no way for everyone to see the whole pipeline, including progress, expectations, and status.

Unfortunately, a lot of companies that purport to offer solutions like the one I've sketched out come up short because they don't necessarily know enough about how to design for process optimization. This leaves companies investing in tools that lead only to the illusion of process improvement for customers and employees. What about the human engagement? What about the employee's experiences in their own day-to-day work? It is not all about the technology.

THE ANSWER

So, what's the answer?

Companies need to commit to real change. They need to stop throwing money into approaches that only go an inch deep and a mile wide. They need to walk the walk and have the political courage to implement real change.

They are going to have to provide employees with quality interfaces. By "quality" interfaces, I mean interfaces that are, technology-wise, from the 21st century. It is essential that companies give employees tools that are comparable in capability to the tools they use in their everyday lives. Employees all have fast, user-friendly, easily navigable, and beautifully designed smartphones now. It is embarrassing for a company if their employees have to fuck around with technology from the 90s.

They are also going to have to implement solutions that

break down siloed functional units so that employees and customers alike can see where processes could use improvement.

Funnily enough, a while back, Domino's Pizza implemented a handy little way to offer customers insight into the status of their pizza delivery. I can track my pizza online and see when and by whom it is made, when it is boxed, when it is en route, and when it should be at my door. Domino's allows me, the customer, a view of the process and where the work is being done...all just for a pizza!

Domino's pizza tracker is an overly simplified example of why it is important for employees and customers alike to have insight into processes. But imagine if customers could track the progress of the really important things in their lives? What if they could do this for their home loan or their incident ticket for their broken laptop? It would lead to a more transparent process.

It would be fantastic if the lender I work with could implement something like Domino's did when I apply for a home loan. But instead, I have to go through filling out all of my data on outdated application forms, then hand over all of my paper documentation. Then, I have to wait a couple of days for them to get back to me. Inevitably, they will need more paperwork and a laundry list of other things. Then, I'll return all of the stuff they've asked for and I'll wait for another week. Maybe a week or two later, I'll get a question about transaction X or purchase Y. We might go back and forth for a while about this, and then, finally, the loan processing will resume. But imagine if I could get a glimpse into where my loan was in the process? I could see, before they even tell me, that they need another copy of Document A and that I forgot a signature on Document B. I could send those documents in without having to wait. The process would take a fraction as long.

That is how it should work, but it doesn't because that loan has to cross silos and necessitates participation of so many different people in so many different departments. The underwriting team has to be talking to loan origination, and loan origination needs to be talking to loan servicing. None of the groups is talking to the customer. But, they should be! They should all be approaching their processes through the lens of the customer. Then, they could create more of a holistic employee and customer experience-driven approach.

To a customer, this solution makes a lot of sense. This is because we see the life of that loan as a whole chain, from our initial contact with an agent all the way through to us receiving that completed loan. Employees within companies, however, see that loan as going through a bunch of different departments that are not in sync with each other, like a bunch of loose chain links that aren't connected.

If the processes aren't good, and they aren't linked in a chain, then the end result is bad. Both the employee experience and the customer experience turn sour.

Companies try to remedy broken processes through small patches here and there. But the problem is that most of their fixes are myopic; they patch small holes in specific departments. But these changes only really affect a small part of the process pipeline. A lot of time, that small patch will happen at the front-end, where the customer is. But it never ends up empowering employees. What companies need to do is to understand the cascade effect; when they can properly fix back-end processes, the front-end processes will work well.

RELUCTANCE

Why are companies so reluctant to institute real change in their quest to offer a good experience?

In a sentence, it's about status quo bias and broken leadership.

Status Quo Bias

I think most employees, especially those in the executive officer ranks, have very good intentions. Those executives absolutely want the company to operate the best it can for the benefit of the customers, the employees, and the shareholders. I think that they are very, *very* sincere about this at the end of the day.

In order to achieve those aspirations, executives talk and think a lot about how they can help their employees help their customers. But the primary issue with this is that, as you move down the ranks of the company, the sincere desire to make change for the better dwindles. By the time it reaches the bottom, it is almost non-existent. Why is this the case?

The sincere quest for improvement can get lost in middle management. In many situations, middle managers want to maintain the status quo as a vehicle for self-preservation in their position or sphere of control. For that reason, many are motivated to be skeptical of change or anything else that might challenge their mental model of the way they believe things should be done, or that is likely to interfere with their own bias.

When executives come into their departments wanting to change specific processes, middle managers become very paranoid. They do not like anyone poking around. That is because they do not want to risk any skeletons being pulled out of the closet or expose weaknesses; this might be punitive to them. They fear getting things wrong and failing. It's human psychology 101.

If something does go wrong in their departments, instead of being forthright and saying, "Hey, I made a mistake," or "Hey, I'd like to get some other opinions on this because we need to do it better," managers tend to shut up and try to hide the situation or downplay it. Instead, if they discussed the issue and showed vulnerability, problems could be fixed or even avoided altogether. Ideally, a middle manager could say something like, "Hey, listen, I screwed up. I've made this mistake a couple of times, and instead of hiding that fact and pretending I didn't mess up, I learned from it. It was actually great that I made that mistake. In fact, before making it again, I was able to catch myself early, talk through it with my colleagues, and we ended up saving $2 million."

But the best way for them to avoid making mistakes is to do nothing, and likely obfuscate the problem. After all, no one gets fired for doing nothing.

Middle managers are very sensitive to any criticism about the processes that they have put in place. For many middle managers, their processes are their brainchildren. The success of their processes are what, they believe, will help them climb the rungs of the corporate ladder. So, when leaders come in with an earnest desire to fix processes, they are often thwarted by middle managers and their ambition.

I worked on a project for a large healthcare company with a third-party team that was responsible for implementing what would be a revolutionary business offering for the client. The third-party team was adamant that they were going to implement the project in a certain way. They basically told my team and me, "This isn't a democracy, and this is how it's going to go." They didn't really care or even know if that specific way was the best path or not. They wanted to do it that way, and *that* was *that*. Echoes of some of my own mis-steps.

The third-party team never implemented a timeline, yet they continued to make commitments that were nearly impossible for them to attain. They missed deadlines, and on the rare occasion that they were able to get their work in on time, it was done haphazardly.

I agree that if you want to get things done, heavy democracies within organizations in the absence of real leadership are overrated. But for this particular project, things started failing, and the third-party team never turned to us to ask for our opinions. Their leaders didn't think to look to see what they could do to remedy the situation. They didn't open up their processes to inspection, and they didn't seek consultation. They should have looked for a consensus about what was going wrong. By "consensus," I do not mean that they needed to get everyone to agree. Rather, they needed to look for the best answer to what the problem was and how to go about fixing it.

But the team leader refused to even acknowledge the problem. He couldn't get over his bias; he was motivated to not acknowledge the problem and not to make changes. He didn't want to lose his position of power or be viewed as weak. In the end, rather than accepting blame, the leaders put the blame on everything else under the sun. The project failed miserably.

I've seen this phenomenon happen everywhere, but it happens more frequently in larger organizations. That is because larger organizations are more decentralized and do not have the support systems in place to acknowledge that reality. Decentralization often leads to a tragedy of the commons effect where, because the organization is so big, there are so many players, and no visibility, the buck gets passed. No one can point to anyone else and say that they didn't get it done because, well, no one got it done.

Leadership, especially in the middle manager ranks, is missing in action. That is because in many cases, middle management is made up of people who were promoted because they were good individual contributors and developed an insatiable craving to move up as quickly as they could. Unfortunately, just because someone was a good individual contributor does not mean that they will be any good at leading or managing people. An immeasurable number of problems come about because of this misconception.

Tensions rise, and employees get frustrated with inept managers. When employees get frustrated with their managers, they have no real option of where to go for help, except for human resources.

Human resources represents the human capital of the business. In theory, they're supposed to be the ones that any employee can go to if he or she has a problem. They're supposed to be the group that he or she can talk to and/ or express frustrations to. But, all too often, people in HR are normally the biggest tattletales of the organization.

For instance, say Bob goes to HR to talk about the issues that he is having with his manager. Bob thinks he is telling his story in confidence, but the moment Bob leaves the HR department, HR sends his boss an email about his complaints.

Part of the reason why the typical HR person does this is to ingratiate themselves with the business managers and hiring managers so that they aren't viewed as contributing to problems within the organization or being wastes of space. They do not want to be affiliated with employees who are viewed as "subversive." They need to maintain good relationships to keep their jobs.

But there is a bigger picture issue here. Bob didn't realize that HR organizations are built to serve the needs of the organization, not the needs of the employees. Helping the employee with real conflict resolution is just *not* HR's gig. Their gig is to be able to onboard people quicker, terminate people faster, and get benefit documents and the like up more efficiently. Their fiduciary responsibility is to the organization, not to the employees.

By and large, employees have to deal with broken leadership without any support. When employees feel like the company does not support them, they become unhappy. When employees aren't happy, they often do not treat customers well.

PEOPLE TRULY WANT TO MAKE OTHERS HAPPY

People truly like to make other people happy; it's human nature. It makes us feel good to help others. When it's all said and done, this is also true in the employee and customer relationship. Employees earnestly want to make their customers happy. They want to do the best jobs of their life every time they have the opportunity to do so. If an employee is happy and is performing elegant and efficient work that meets the needs of their bosses and delights their customers, there will be a positive effect on the customer.

If, on the other hand, an employee is constrained, is as in the dark as the customer, is not authorized to do things to delight customers, does not trust his manager, can't provide information the way the customer would expect it to be provided, or can't provide guidance or visibility, then he or she becomes immensely frustrated. I can describe this frustration only as an employee hanging up after a call with a customer and thinking, "What the hell am I doing here? I can't do anything. I can't solve any problem."

Like I said, I believe people truly want to help others. Employees are simply trying to mimic that feeling of helping one customer, and scaling it to help all of their customers. There are many variables that must be understood in order to achieve that, but if employees are given the agency to understand those variables, then they can offer that fabulous experience every time. If companies can create an environment where innovation and constructive nonconformity are present, then the sky's the limit in terms of delivering customer experience.

THE SKY'S THE LIMIT

I truly believe that *the sky's the limit* for customer experience. Companies could pull light-years ahead of the competition by offering new products, new services, and better value in the realm of customer experience.

There is massive room for growth in customer experience in all industries. But there are industries like the airline industry that could really take it to the limit for all passengers, not just the ones with top-tier status. For instance, when my flight is delayed, why do I have to call American Airlines? Couldn't they have already worked to fix my reservations without me calling in or waiting in a line that's fifty people deep at the counter? They already know that my flight is delayed. Why can't they go ahead and take the steps to get me on another flight? They could take it a step further and inform my rental car company or my hotel of my late arrival. But they don't. It "isn't their job," and they don't have the capability to do it.

It really isn't that hard to go the extra mile. But companies don't recognize that they even have the option to go that extra distance. And since they don't recognize it, they might never get there.

I think that American Express actually does recognize the long road ahead and is taking strides to get there. They do a pretty decent job of offering customer service that goes above and beyond. In fact, they are able to not only react to a customer request, but actually be proactive about it. For example, not only can customer service agents help you get a great concert ticket, but they also think about all of the other things that you will need before and after the concert. American Express agents can work to get you a rental car to get you to the concert, a dinner reservation for after the concert, and a hotel room to stay in that night. Their agents are empowered to go a step further to offer a great customer experience. However, Amex also realizes that the world is changing, and that there is a younger generation that has different wants than their current offerings. Amex knows that there never will be a finish line, *ever*. Amex will have to keep at it!

These days, technology is widely available for workers across all industries to go the extra mile. For instance, why do loan officers sit behind their desks at their branch office waiting for applicants? They should be at open houses holding their iPads and handing out their business cards to potential buyers. They could process potential buyers right then and there, and get their application info in the system.

There are thousands of ways to get better, but first things first: Companies need to fix their broken processes and understand the positive correlation between employee experience and customer experience.

WHERE DO WE GO FROM HERE?

In this chapter and the two previous ones, we've cataloged the primary issues that plague organizations. In the following chapters, we will explore various tactics (and the philosophy behind them) to improve and optimize the employee experience and, ultimately, the customer experience. These tactics are tried and true, and bolstered by science.

We will explore ways to help managers and employees alike, who have simply given up because they've tried for so long to affect change, but have never been able to. Perhaps they feel as though they've spent their careers pushing Jell-O up a wall. Perhaps they've become jaded and decided that they aren't going to bother anymore.

I am here to reinvigorate those who want to do better by

imparting my and my colleagues' hard-earned experiences, demonstrating a new way to change, and showing them the tools that will get them there. This book will help organizations transform themselves into institutions that are admired and trusted by their customers and their employees.

PART TWO

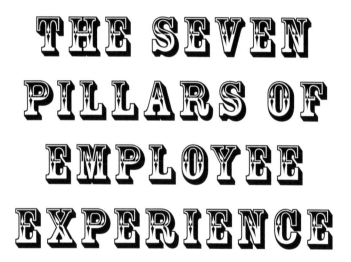

THE SEVEN PILLARS OF EMPLOYEE EXPERIENCE

AUTHORIZATION TO ACT

What is *authorization to act*? We can explore the concept in a story about Jane. Jane is a manager in the billing department at a company. She is one of the "process leaders" tasked with representing business interests, looking at the flow and movement of work, monitoring the touch points of the customer journey, and making sure processes are optimized.

She has been given accountability, but no real authorization to act or make decisions. If a decision must be made for Jane's department, she takes it to someone above her. Then, she will demur or defer to that person's decision—even if she disagrees—because she doesn't want to take the risk of fighting or losing a battle.

What is happening to Jane is a widespread problem. People like Jane are told that they're in charge of their department, or a specific project, and are held accountable to its success, but their authorization to act isn't real, as demonstrated by the employees not feeling safe to do so.

Authorization to act happens when a company gives their employees the power to act and determine how to best approach their responsibilities. Many companies promote the fact that they give their employees the authorization to act, and some companies even have it stated in their mission statement. The problem, though, is that companies don't actually give their employees the authorization to act. Rather, what companies actually do is give their employees *accountability*.

Holding employees *accountable* without giving them the *authorization to act* is not right. Employees should not be held *accountable* for their actions if they aren't given any power to dictate or influence what their actions are. For example, I am sure that more than one of the 5,300 Wells Fargo employees who were fired for opening fake bank accounts did not want to open fake banking accounts for moral and ethical reasons. But without being given any authority to act, they couldn't question the righteousness or effectiveness of the action. They were told to follow the policy and procedure of the organization. I have to believe that most of those employees wanted to act differently, but didn't have the confidence to say anything. Or perhaps they feared they might lose their jobs if they stood up and said something. In the end, we discovered that was exactly what happened. They did lose their jobs because the bank suffered losses from what they did.

For Jane, her bosses told her that they wanted her to run accounts receivable and lead a project to increase the velocity of capturing revenue and reduce the need to rework incorrect invoices. Jane had to complete the process definition for a future state, truly understand the historical performance, and find root cause(s) for the reasons why defective invoices were occurring. Although she couldn't get the historical performance data, she did discover that one of the major causal problems occurred during the handoff between policy servicing and accounts receivable. She realized that incorrect changes were being made in policy servicing and by the time the invoices reached billing, it was too late to correct those mistakes before the invoice went out. When she told her department head about her findings, Jane was told that policy servicing wasn't part of her remit to change, and that she needed to work around the issue. She was told that she wasn't authorized to reach out to the policy servicing department.

The problem is, without instituting changes in policy

servicing, there was little to no chance Jane could pull off any real benefit. She had no authority to make the decisions necessary to meet the goals, and yet she was still held accountable. Her managers had only paid her lip service.

Why is this type of behavior harmful?

When someone like Jane is given accountability without the authority to make decisions, decision-making tends to become very consensus-driven. Instead of Jane owning her project and implementing what she believes is the best solution, she schedules endless meetings and escalates every single decision to someone higher up in the organization to make sure that her fingerprints aren't the only ones on the gun. This is commonly known as a CYA mentality. CYA stands for "Cover Your Ass." Jane creates layers and layers of meetings and emails and escalations, which slows the process down and allows her to cover her ass if things go wrong. She does this because she doesn't feel politically safe.

A decision will get made by someone higher up in the organization, but usually that person has little to no deep understanding of the department. Therefore, Jane, the person who is intimately involved in her organization and is the one who knows the best solution for her team, just acquiesces to whatever that alpha personality says to her in the meeting. Then, she shuts her mouth and goes along with the decision. And guess what? Most of the time, the project fails to meet expectations because the best person with the best idea (in this case, Jane) feared making the decision and pulling the trigger.

In the bigger picture of things, the customer suffers. There is not a single employee who would stick out his or her neck in order to help a customer if it meant going against the decision made, even if the employee truly wanted to, as I believe everyone would. Why is that so? Because the company can't fire the customer, demote him, fine him, or move him to Siberia never to be seen again. But the company can do these things to employees.

At the end of the day, the employee isn't willing to risk their ass for a customer. At this point, that is no longer called customer experience, nor is it called customer service. It's called "not my problem."

BUT ISN'T IT TRUE THAT NO DECISION SHOULD BE MADE LIGHTLY?

Some might wonder if it isn't a good thing that Jane is forced to be careful in weighing every decision and asking everyone around her for their opinion. Yes, of course every decision should be made with deliberate thought and the proper intention behind it. But the problem is that Jane and others act cautiously, not because they want to get the best solution, but because they are so damned fearful of failure and retribution.

This fear trickles down onto employees on the frontlines of the processing centers and customer-contact centers— the employees who interact directly with customers. It overwhelms them and negatively affects how they deal with customers.

This fear cuts across businesses and industries. It results in customer service representatives not wanting to take accountability to help customers. Some companies have created an environment where employees are so fearful of failure that, rather than trying to help customers and risk failing, they would rather tell customers, in so many words, to screw off. You see this in companies that have a stronghold within a particular industry. For example, in companies like Time Warner Cable/Spectrum, Sprint, Comcast, AT&T, and Verizon, employees are so full of fear that they would rather act like complete assholes to customers than make a call on implementing a solution and risking failure.

This behavior hurts the customer and ultimately hurts the business. But still, employees are implicitly told that if they screw up, they're gone.

The sky will not fall if an employee takes charge and makes a mistake. They need to be given the authority to make calls and feel safe if they make a wrong one.

AUTHORIZING ACTION

How can companies communicate to their employees that they have true authorization to act?

Bosses need to straight up tell their employees that they are allowed to take action, and that it is okay if they get "it" wrong. Managers and supervisors have to show vulnerability about decisions made in their own careers to ensure that their employees really feel empowered to be authentic. There must be an element of support between bosses and employees—not hand-holding, but real, unyielding support. The support structure must be based on trust. Employees need to be able to trust that their bosses have their backs and, in turn, bosses need to trust that their employees can get the job done. Like they were hired to do! Bosses need to tell their employees that they can and should do their job, and that the only time they need to ask for advice from their superiors is when they feel truly cornered. When there is an honest support structure in place, employees will *want* to take the reins.

Money can also work, but to a lesser extent. Some

companies use monetary incentives to demonstrate to their employees that they have the authority to act. Some companies give out bonuses, spiffs, stock options, and the like so that employees feel rewarded in the success of the company and therefore want to get things done.

When employees are given the authority to act, incredible things happen. I've seen it occur so many times in my own company and within those that I work with.

At BP3, we are successful in part because we have told every employee in every area of the business that he or she has authority to act. *To do the right thing.* Whatever he or she needs to do to help make the customer successful, we tell them to fucking do it. Nobody will get fired for trying to do the right thing.

For instance, if our engineers want to talk to customers to see what they think about a particular new feature, the engineers have the authority to pick up the phone and call any one of our clients to validate direction. We want them to develop their own relationships outside of just their own implementation and support teams.

In most organizations, this is unheard of. Rarely do you ever see someone in product allowed to talk to a customer. He would have to go through someone in sales or account management, and have them act as a middleman. By allowing our developers to talk to customers as they please without an intermediary or a babysitter in the form of a salesperson or account manager, we are inherently telling them that they have the authority to act! We're holding them accountable for their job *and* allowing them to do it to the best of their ability. And what comes of it? A better product and a happier customer.

SILOS PREVENT AUTHORIZATION TO ACT

In companies like BP3 that hold employees accountable *and authorize employees to act*, things play out in a completely different way than how things played out with Jane as we described them at the beginning of the chapter. BP3 and other like-minded companies allow leaders to make decisions with confidence and authority.

But this can only happen if a leader has holistic access and insight into what happens before and after his individual contribution to the process. This means that if a product manager wants to make decisions about the product, he must be able to understand what happens to the product in all areas of the business. He must be able to see the entire picture. He must understand how the salespeople and marketing folks interact with the product. But in most companies, the departments are siloed, what happens in each silo is obfuscated, and the product manager has no idea what is happening to the product as it moves from one department to the next. It would be ideal if the product were truly "owned" by the product manager, but unfortunately, the product cuts across the business from siloed unit to siloed unit, and constraints are everywhere.

Siloing creates boundaries between employees; intentions and messages get screwed up. For instance, in the case of the developer who has to go through a salesperson to speak to a customer, the customer's intentions will only reach the developer through the salesperson's filter. If I am a developer working on a program to improve operational processes for Business X, and I hear about what the customer wants only through a business analyst or the head sales guy on an account who is working as the intermediary, I'm never truly hearing anything directly from the target consumer. How do I know that an intermediary is providing me with unbiased, unprejudiced information? How can I be sure that he hasn't processed the information given to him by the consumer through his own mental model and through his internal filter? It has basically turned into the telephone game where developers are at the mercy of whomever has taken his role as intermediary and made himself the "expert" at what the consumer wants.

In this case, the voice of an intermediary or any other

"customer expert" is worth shit. As a developer, I need to hear what the consumer of the product wants directly from the consumer. In their own words and in their own vernacular—direct, unfiltered, unadulterated, and unbiased.

But when I don't have the authority to act and reach out to the customer myself, I have to deal with this intermediary. Thus begins a process of me having to negotiate with a middleman about what I think the customer wants, and what the best thing for the customer is.

There is a growing awareness about the problem with siloing, but people don't really understand the implications when it comes specifically to the employee and customer experience. When negotiation begins between silos, the customer's voice gets lost. So, companies must find a way around negotiation. What companies need to do is to understand the value of collaboration in their quest to offer a great employee and customer experience.

CHAPTER 5

COLLABORATION

There is an important distinction between a collaborative work environment and a negotiation-based work environment.

In a collaborative work environment, all groups that the process cuts across are represented. In the previous chapter, if an intermediary and the developer worked in a collaborative work environment, they would feel equally authorized to act and make decisions. They would be able to work to find a consensus (aka the best answer) for the customer. They would be allowed to take accountability and pivot if they found a better way to deliver a good customer experience. They would begin to think in terms of the final outcome: Is the customer happier? They would get to think outside of their little world and get to focus on things more important than their SLAs, whether their bosses are pleased, or whether they might get fired for failing.

Unfortunately, intermediaries and the developer live in the same negotiation-based work environment as Jane does. In their worlds, they are held accountable but are not authorized to act. Jane is not able to look outside of her department to find the best solution. If, for instance, she was tasked with changing a process that had to do with customer feedback, she would be dissuaded by management to go and solicit help from the team that receives customer feedback. Even if she did seek their guidance, the customer feedback group would not want to spend their time or resources to help. That group would see Jane's problem as *her problem*, not *their problem*, so why help her?

When a company is siloed like that, it becomes a "me" against "you" sort of environment. Each team sees themselves as a separate entity, where they have their own budget, their own SLAs, their own wants and needs, and their own filter through which they view the customer. They shape and manipulate data to what is amenable to them: their organization and their mission, their charter and their goals. This leads to friction within the company because each organization tends to have different opinions about what the customer needs and wants. Because different departments have different opinions about customers, when it comes time to execute for that customer, no one can agree on how to do it. The various departments, therefore, begin to negotiate about what they think is best.

When teams negotiate, they are forced to compromise. This leads to watered down projects that are left sterile because all of the value has been compromised away. Negotiation, as a form of compromise, is more about degrees of losing than succeeding. In that type of negotiation-based work environment, no one wins, especially not the customer.

Departments should not negotiate. They need to collaborate. By taking a collaborative approach, there will be no tension about who does what or whose voice is heard; everyone gets a say, everyone shares the costs, and everyone works together.

But in order for companies to get to the point where customer problems are solved through collaboration rather than negotiation, they need to deal with the underlying problem of silos. I hate using the word "silos" to describe various functional areas of an organization because it is such a negative term, but damn, it's just what they are.

Each functional area within an organization has their

own biases, motivations, and desires, and each silo fights against other silos for resources. When it comes to the value chain of a company, whether it is Ford or Amazon, everyone is fighting for resources that end up getting distributed either evenly or unevenly across the organization.

In the end, no one ends up reaping the benefits or getting the yield. Everyone just ends up getting pissed off at one another because they feel like their projects are colliding with each other's in the quest for resources. Project collisions occur when different siloed departments have to fight each other for resources and power.

COLLABORATION CAN BE DONE!

David Skomo said that he didn't even "realize that he was in a silo" until he moved to a matrix organization and finally saw the value that a collaborative work environment brought to customers and employees alike. The matrix aspect of the organization is a result of a culture journey that those within the company have committed themselves to. Five central core beliefs act as its cornerstone.

Those five central core beliefs were written by those in the very top executive level of the company that David works at. David keeps the five core beliefs on his desk, close by. He says that their culture values are "integrity, compassion, relationships, innovation, and performance." He says that relationships sit in the middle because that is the linchpin that propels their culture. Of course, David joked that it can't be done in one day. "You don't just come in one day with a poster, put it up on the wall, and say, 'That's our culture right over there. Just look at that. Read that everyday. That's our culture.'"

It takes an ongoing journey to promote those values, especially that central value of relationships, which help to break down siloed structures. In order to promote those relationships among the members of the company, the company David works at has town hall meetings at various levels of the organization. They remotely invite all employees to join video conferences to meet with the leadership and hear about strategic objectives and recent organizational changes, and to give them a chance to submit questions.

David conducts town halls of his own to better connect with employees on the frontlines. He organizes them so that the people on the frontlines can talk about the things that really matter to them. These types of things break down that "me vs. you" mentality that siloed organizations engender.

David talked about the incredible things that can come

out of that connected environment. David wanted to improve customer experience, namely the Net Promoter Score, and took a page out of the company's book, where cross-functional meetings are the norm. He reached out across traditional department divides to recruit help for his mission.

David was "amazed by the willingness of others within the organization" to pitch in and help, and literally drop everything and come in physically to remote meetings to address the situation at hand.

David was getting messages from other executives about their suggestions and opinions, and he suddenly realized that he could attack the problem cross-functionally and make sure that the entire organization was on the same page. They became aligned on the strategy to drive NPS. No longer were they thinking of things only in the realm of their own departments. They shared everyone's results across the organization. They were open to hear from everyone. They shared strategies, watched how they played out, and learned from each other. They observed how one part of the business could impact the success of another.

David said that the main takeaway from that lesson was that he didn't need to be afraid to call out people in other parts of the company. He said that if he realized that what someone was doing was negatively impacting his own org., he could address the issue. He figured out that other executives were happy to work together with him to fix any problem.

David said that the teams are stronger because they collaborate. They've been able to get results faster and have a stronger impact. He said that he's also gained respect from other colleagues in the organization that he wouldn't necessarily have expected to, because he reached out for help and leveraged it.

REMEDYING PROJECT COLLISIONS

How can companies remedy the problem of project collisions by working through projects collaboratively like David was able to? It's all a matter of will. Executives cannot just talk about how they want collaboration; they have to really engage and show the courage to make structural changes up and down the chain to mitigate negotiation and collisions, and promote collaboration and communication. They must find ways to get the whole organization on board with one goal and allow them a way to communicate their needs.

Dawie Oliver found a way to communicate a singular

message across his whole organization so that everyone was on the same page. Dawie Oliver is the CIO of Westpac New Zealand, a 4,500-person organization that is a part of a 150-year old, 32,000-person organization called Westpac Group. Dawie was featured in a great article written by Chris Cancialosi for *Forbes* titled "How Culture Change Fuels Digital Transformation: Lessons From Westpac New Zealand" about the prolific work he did at Westpac. Dawie was generous enough to sit down with me for this book.

When the subject of collaboration versus negotiation came up, I was so goddamned impressed by how Dawie promoted communication and collaboration among his teams. When I asked Dawie what tools he found most helpful, he responded that he didn't use fancy tools or the common channels. He found success through something much simpler.

He said that his golden ticket was "My time and my voice, and the time and voices of my leadership, and the time and voices of our teams." In Dawie's particular case, the project that he wanted everyone to get on board with was changing the culture. Dawie envisioned a culture that married the vision of the business to the aspirations of the teams.

So Dawie went back to basics, so that the message of

cultural change would permeate throughout the business. He spoke about the message "unwaveringly" dozens of times "in as many different forms as possible." He's had dozens and dozens of conversations in front of large groups, in front of small groups, in the bathroom, at the water cooler, and in the elevator, explaining himself over and over again. "Nothing," he says, "drives change like a great story told in person."

Dawie wanted to make sure that the message was *communicated* rather than *broadcasted*. To Dawie, communication was preferred because it allowed a dialogue where everyone could be included, which promoted collaboration.

Dawie said that for him, tooling and technology brought up the caboose of the culture change train. Dawie says that he often gets invited to tell his transformation story in front of other organizations (even some competitors!). He says, "When the invite comes, the words used in it are very telling." He says, "If the invite [asks me] to come and share our Agile Transformation Journey, then most likely, they missed the point of what we are doing." They don't understand that collaboration and communication brought the change, not fancy tooling, or Agile and Lean methods. They don't get that "Agile" and "Lean" are results of the behaviors that they instill because they contain the practices that support the desired behaviors—they are not the cause of them.

Today's world is all about communication and collaboration. The problem, though, is that while sometimes you can create a positive and healthy collaborative environment, you can still make bad decisions that yield bad outcomes. In order to prevent that from happening, you need to ensure that your collaborative environment is also one that practices the concept of failing fast.

FAILING FAST

"Failing fast" is a common term in entrepreneurial circles. It is a technique where a company proves the efficacy of an idea by trying it. In "failing fast," companies don't just talk endlessly about ideas; they actually implement them to see if they can prove that they work. When they don't work, they pack up and pivot—hence the "fast" part of the phrase.

Failing fast is nearly impossible for some companies to do. Even if a CEO wants to try something new, it's so hard to move a giant corporation—it's like using a four-foot long rudder to turn a 1,000-foot long vessel. It takes time. That's why so few companies are able to practice "failing fast."

For others, they've never seen the need to practice

failing fast. They like the status quo and don't want to risk anything.

Typically, companies only feel desperate in their need to change when their market gets disrupted. At BP3, we've worked with large energy companies in the oil and gas industry. They were willing to change, but only because their industry was hit hard. Their industry was burning, and their shit was on fire (not literally billowing smoke like a "burning bucket of death on fire," but rather crashing and burning economically), so they had to get a lot smarter very quickly about how they operated in this new reality. That's why they came to us to help them change.

Unfortunately, for many companies, if their shit isn't on fire, they think it's okay to just glide. Employees and process leaders don't feel the need to act, decision-ing becomes inert, which kills all velocity and productivity, and no one is willing to throw real money or power into R&D and innovation.

Sometimes I see companies that claim they are committed to taking steps to change even when their industry isn't on fire. But there is no real incentive to change. All they do is talk about change. They do a lot of pontificating and theorizing, and a lot of mental masturbation around the "what if's." They end up doing a lot of theorycrafting.

Theorycrafting happens when individuals within companies talk about improvements, but never take the actual steps to bring anything to fruition.

I've worked with companies that, in theory, like the idea of failing fast. But they won't actually implement it in reality. I see it everywhere. For instance, I worked with the enterprise architecture group at a retail-pharma company. They wanted to create a whole new business model within pharmacy, and the enterprise architects wanted to own the technical implementation of that vision. They had created a very nice PowerPoint that outlined their plans, which they liked to show off...a lot.

But in the end, nothing came of it! They talked about the PowerPoint for two damned years! There was no initiative to prove anything out—to implement a small portion of Layer X or test out Process Z. They tried to sell the initiative to other departments in the company, but when they were asked about trial data to back up their claims, they didn't have any! They were never able to gather any data because they never used the fail fast mentality in implementing their concept in the first place!

The other departments were not convinced, and they pushed back at the enterprise architects. When the business guys asked them, "Does this really work?" the architecture team told them it would take some time—like three to five years—just to implement it before they could even begin to see if it would work!

The business guys were not impressed. They knew that by the time they implemented and figured out if the system would work, the market would have changed. Another company would have come out and created the solution, while these guys were still tweaking the font on their PowerPoints.

The business guys reached out to BP3, and we built them a working prototype in ten weeks. No one shit on it. The business guys thought it was really impressive and wanted to evolve it. So they took it to their enterprise architecture guys, to get them on board. The architecture guys realized that they had fucked up by stating that it would take three to five years to complete their system. So, they pushed back on our creation and told the business guys that their vision had been "different" from the solution we created.

That was complete rubbish. Our model was pragmatic, and we had built it in ten weeks compared to their three to five years. We had proved them wrong. The enterprise architecture guys told the business guys and us to "Do what we wanted," but that they would continue to build out their "vision," which was by and large the same as ours. Designing two systems would be stupid and useless. At best, the pharma company would have two duplicate systems within the organization, but most likely, neither would survive. *Politics.*

But the architecture guys dug their heels in and blocked our solution from being implemented, so nothing ever came of it. In the end, our solution would have put medicine in the hands of patients. Their PowerPoint would never fucking do that; have you ever seen a PowerPoint deck produce a product? Nope, me either, not one single time in the long, sad history of PowerPoint decks.

That is what failing fast is about. That is what we do at BP3. That is our mission. We implement solutions. And if we find they don't work, we stop and pivot to a better solution. We don't theorycraft around PowerPoints.

THE IMPORTANCE OF A-B TESTING IN FAILING FAST

Failing fast is all about trying to prove something as quickly as you can. The way you can do that is through A-B testing. A-B testing is what actually separates fact from fiction. A-B testing is when actors input different solution paradigms or patterns into a funnel, go through the rigor of testing them, and then validate them. If the solution works, then great! If it doesn't, actors move to the next potential solution through the ringer immediately. A-B testing is part of the "fast" in fail fast.

A-B testing is the actualization of an idea to validate its efficacy. There are no PowerPoints or diagrams. That is all bullshit. A-B testing is just about putting your idea to work and seeing what happens. You can deal with things like scalability, data duplication, unification, etc., as they arise. But for now, orchestrate something and do it *today*.

Most importantly, A-B testing is in the spirit of encouraging mistakes instead of trying to avoid them. The goal is actually to *make mistakes*.

From there, you can gather information about how an organization needs to change or pivot based on what you see.

A-B testing is helpful because it allows all different types of learners the chance to understand what the outcome is when a specific idea is implemented. Some people are visual learners, others are auditory, and others are tactile. Through A-B testing, employees can see and understand a complete and real picture of the possibility of each proposed initiative. A-B testing goes beyond theorycrafting, project plans, PowerPoint decks, and spreadsheets.

FAILING FAST IN REAL TIME

Dawie enacted a "fail fast" mentality in his company in order to catalyze change. It was wildly successful, but it took him a while before he understood just how beneficial failing fast was.

Dawie was first acquainted with "fail fast" when he was a relatively senior executive at Standard Bank in South Africa, before he moved to Westpac. Dawie and his team were struggling with an IT conversion. The project was hitting the classic IT conversion hurdles; IT conversion was coming in over budget, late, and not doing what it needed to do. He spent between eighteen months and two years trying to get it right.

Dawie said he was trying to get it to dance, but only managed to get it "shuffling a bit quicker." Then, one day, a direct report came to him and presented the idea of Agile process (fail fast is a concept of Agile). Dawie shut him down. He told his report, "That's not the kind of stuff that we do around here, we're a bank." The report persisted, taking Dawie for a drink and explaining the benefits of Agile to him.

The report convinced Dawie to try an initial experiment. The results of what Dawie saw converted him into a believer. The whole practice of trying that first experiment only reinforced for him the whole point of failing fast and iterating.

Dawie said that what struck him most about the benefits of Agile was that it centered around human behavior rather than mechanical or scientific theories. Agile process was, he realized, about people. It was about respect for people and respect for their views, contributions, and opinions. It allowed people to throw around their ideas and follow their intuitions through A-B testing. It allowed people to not be afraid of failing. It allowed people to learn through doing and through failing. Dawie says that he doesn't like to use the term "agile," but prefers to think of it as "learner's mind." He says, "Dogma is the enemy of learning."

The South African bank where Dawie worked experimented with Agile, and it turned out to be so successful that it has now become a part of the ethos of the entire bank.

Dawie continues to study the subject of Agile. Some of his favorite thinkers on the subject are Steve Bell, who wrote *Lean IT*, Rebecca Parsons, the CTO of ThoughtWorks (and one of the most influential voices in tech), and Jez Humble, who wrote *Continuous Delivery*.

When Dawie was hired at Westpac, he saw similar issues as those he had seen at Standard Bank. He saw Westpac as a technology organization that was massively dysfunctional. The burning platform for Westpac, he realized, wasn't the industry or the banking aspect of the business, but rather the flailing technology side. The employees didn't have the proper technology to fight the good fight.

Westpac was operating on legacy systems that were just not cutting it, and Dawie needed to fix the situation fast. Some would argue that there is no way to go about changing a legacy system or how you run it, but Dawie and his team are proof that is just not true. They did it within a 150-year-old company!

How did he do it? By utilizing "fail fast."

People who run enterprise systems and large mainframes operate in an old school way. They argue that they can have only quarterly releases, and that they have to test all of the releases together and implement afterward. But when they do that and something breaks, it's very difficult to start looking for the break in the code. This creates massive problems for companies.

So Dawie changed the game and challenged his developers to release updates and new iterations early and often, and provided them plenty of expert support as to *how* they might do it. When you do that, it is okay if you fail (if there is a bug in the code, for example) because mistakes are cheap and easy to manage when you release small amounts of code frequently. Risk management becomes realistic when you adopt "high velocity, small increment" fixes.

Dawie says that, oftentimes, his developers release daily. Their longest release cycle is a month, but his employees have taken responsibility for this, and are working to bring the release cycle down.

His teams are not afraid to innovate and test and fail. This has made the cadence of change faster. This wasn't the desired end result for Dawie, but has been a very welcome by-product!

Dawie's "fail fast and fail often" mentality has changed Westpac for the better, and now he fully understands just how important it is.

IMPLICATIONS OF FAILING FAST

Failing fast is so important because companies are more at risk than ever of competitors coming into their space, disrupting their industries, and taking their market share.

Companies don't get that. *They just don't.* If things aren't on fire for them yet, they will be very soon.

I want incumbent companies like old school banks to sit back and think for a second about how fucking easy it would be for Amazon to open a bank. People love Amazon and trust Amazon. Why wouldn't people trust Amazon with basic banking services? They already do a fantastic job at offering other great products! Incumbent banks have nothing; they offer blah level customer service. "But," they say, "We do have point systems! All you have to do is earn 27,000,000 points, and then you can buy an ice pack with the bank's logo on it!"

Amazon will come in and destroy them. Businesses can't keep customers in today's environment because of perceived switching costs. They're going to have to do a hell of a lot better than what they are doing now.

I could sit and ruminate all day long on the possibilities. But basically, what I am saying is that today, there is not a single industry that cannot be disrupted. This has little to do with technology, e-commerce, and the appeal of fancy apps. No, this is more fundamental. Right now, anyone has the ability to affect change in a business model and innovate around that. Incumbent companies need to evolve to compete.

Companies must use fail fast to iterate and determine the best course of action for enacting the necessary change.

Otherwise, it will take them years and years to get where they need to be. They need to do it fast...competition is here.

Macy's, a 100-year-old retailer, has closed a couple of hundred stores. This, to me, signals that they most likely won't be around in five years. Macy's cannot compete with Amazon; they're too late to the game. Macy's didn't innovate. They're siloed and stuck in a rut, and they're soon to be gone. Macy's never adopted a fail fast mentality. In order to get out of the muck, they needed to test and test. They needed to empower groups within the organization to innovate and fail fast.

What would groups like that look like?

There would need to be groups of talented people from various departments. Rarely, though, have I ever seen that. If I do see innovation centers, they are comprised of ten to twelve people who are brainiacs, no doubt, but who are all plucked from one part of the organization. Because they all come from a singular part of the organization, they lack a heterogeneous view. I might see twelve people from the IT department who are responsible for advanced R&D assimilation. But they don't know much of anything about what the customer is buying, why they are buying, or what the customer truly feels like when interacting with the product or the company.

Those twelve IT guys won't know anything about customer feedback because the customer feedback department (almost always the marketing function) has all of their data clogged in their own silo. Siloed departments don't share information with one another. Sometimes that is because they decide not to. Other times, it is because they don't understand what data is important to share. Still other times, it is because they are not allowed to share their data. That is hugely problematic when a company tries to fail fast. They can't make quick yet informed decisions because they don't have a holistic view of what is going on.

We were a part of a project to deploy a critical financial product solution for a big bank. We wanted to know what it typically cost to onboard a customer, but no one could tell us. We went all the way up to the senior vice presidents. They couldn't tell us, either. The financial department would not share the information with them even though they were the senior vice presidents of the division in which we were all working!

We were literally walking around like some kind of value fiends, vibrating at a high frequency, trying to figure out what the fuck was going to make a difference for our innovation project. But ultimately, we couldn't do anything to fail fast and innovate without transparency, visibility, and the correct data. We were unable to prove actionable insights because we were unable to gain access to information that spanned the process from beginning to end.

DO IT FOR THE CUSTOMER

Failing fast impacts the customer as much as the employee. Companies that fail fast are always working to do what is best by the customer, and offer it as quickly as possible. The environment at Westpac is so different from what we saw in Jane's scenario, where she cared too much about negotiation, was not authorized to act, thus demurred and deferred and in the end, nothing was done. She did the opposite of failing fast because she felt like she couldn't make a mistake.

It's not that Jane isn't a good person or doesn't care about the customer. She was forced to suppress her motivation to do the right thing. Because Jane had to think about so many other things, she forgot that she is supposed to work in concert with the vision of the customer.

Fail fast allows the voice of the customer to be heard in decision-making. But this is only possible when a company has a flow of data about what the customer wants and uti-lizes that information to influence change. More and more, companies are able to utilize fail fast methods because they have a constant flow of data about their customers and the insights to act on that data.

UNDERSTANDING AND APPLYING CUSTOMER AND EMPLOYEE INSIGHTS

Data is a very hot topic today. Every company and their mother brags about how much data they have, and how state-of-the-art their data is. They talk a lot about how their data is going to change the world.

Some data will change the world, surely. But most of the time, the data that companies are working to gather is self-serving and not truly insightful or beneficial to the end game: helping the customer.

Personnel are incentivized, paid, viewed, valued, and awarded on the metrics measured by data. But those metrics are internal and have to do with measuring things like cycle time in a call center, time on hold, and one-and-done calls, and have nothing to do with customer experience. They think that if those metrics look good, then everything is A-Okay. Well, they're dead wrong, because those metrics don't necessarily correlate to how customer experience is truly going.

SOME COMPANIES DO DATA RIGHT

Facebook is an example of a company that is committed to gathering high fidelity data so as to have better insight into their employee and customer experience. Gathering this data is embedded into Facebook's very nature. Facebook knows which data matters the most. That ability has made Facebook the best data company out there. It has enabled them to innovate at every turn. They have gone from a small social networking application at colleges to a major player in social communities to a global platform for commerce.

Google is another great example of a company that is dedicated to data. Google understands, almost better than anyone, just what the right kind of data can do for the employee and customer experience. There is a whole book written about how good Google is at it, titled *How Google Works*. That book was a #1 *New York Times* bestseller.

Google gathers so much of the right kind of data on their customers that they know exactly what their customers want. They don't really have to dig deep. They have insight into how customers interact with their products. They measure every click. They measure every page view. They measure every ad. They measure every word typed. All of their measured data has led them to enter new and exciting markets. They started as a search engine, but Google now offers email, Google Docs, smartphones, home devices, VR platforms, and soon, self-driving cars. Their growth is limitless...all thanks to the fact that they know how to measure their data.

Google Maps was created because a team of people realized that customers were searching where to find Place X and how to get there. They realized, through all of this data, that they could offer a simple solution. But it was only possible because that team had access and insight into what data every team at Google was dealing with.

The guys and girls who work at Google are perceived geniuses. They are smart, there is no doubt about it, but the reality is that they aren't geniuses. They aren't creating Einstein-level solutions to difficult problems. They are looking at the environment with all of their data and then trusting their instincts about where and what they should be doing next. They are smart enough to see their data, parse out the important bits, and read a story from it.

Google is also dedicated to offering a fantastic employee experience, and they are able to do this by flipping through appropriate data. They mine for data from the employees just like they mine data from their customers. They do this by design. They've done it since Day 1.

Google is smart; they look at their employees just like they look at their customers, so they know the importance of gathering insight from them. They can see what employees want, what they need, and what they are looking for. Then, Google can adjust accordingly. This has resulted in one of the flattest, most transparent companies that I have ever encountered. The visibility that their employees have makes them feel authorized to act and able to collaborate among different functional departments, and thus, they are able to accomplish what they set out to do.

Google earned the right to be thought of as one of the best in terms of understanding their data. Google walks the walk in regards to data. Other companies, like Uber, only talk the talk. Uber was at the right place at the right time to be able to gather an extraordinary amount of data from their customers. Because Uber has all of this data on their customers and partners (aka drivers), one would think they would know how to use it in order to improve how they operated.

But, from an operational standpoint, Uber is not state-of-the-art. I have a friend who decided to try out driving for UberEats in his spare time. He worked for two weeks but was never paid. Uber has this thing called "Instant Pay," which is really just startup speak for "getting paid electronically right then and there." No matter what you want to call it, *he was not paid after his required driving period ended*, so he emailed the support address, and a support ticket was opened by a guy in India. My friend kept getting bounced around to people who would respond with a template response, "I'm so happy you asked this question, we will let you know when Instant Pay is available for your account!" No one ever answered his question about when he was going to be paid. No one resolved his issue. He got no pay and no explanation, just an automated response. Uber took one of their partners, who is basically also a customer, and threw him around the ringer. My friend was basically told that even though he signed up in good faith and did the work, UberEats didn't care.

My friend noticed that in his support ticket, it said that his problem was "Resolved." Uber concluded that his problem was "Resolved" because they responded. That is how Uber measures "successful" resolutions. With all of the data that Uber has to pull from, they choose to mark a resolution "successful" if it is one and done. Perhaps they thought that by closing out the ticket, the metrics would look good? Remember that Cost per Contact model I discussed? But what are the chances that my friend will ever speak well about Uber again? He hasn't thus far and refuses to use them today.

He made a huge fuss in the tickets—yes, more than one was submitted—then two weeks later, he finally was paid for those first two weeks. Then, he also received a small voucher to order food from UberEats. Jesus.

This is the same problem, whether you are a "Digital Disruptor" company, meaning your whole business origination began with a model of disrupting established industries, or you are an incumbent company who has been around. If you can't measure your data in the right way—for the benefit of the customer—then what the hell are you doing? You are in massive trouble if you can't get it right.

Someone is going to come in and create a threat to you. For Uber, it might be Lyft, or it might be local rideshare companies. Here in Austin, Uber left because they didn't want to play ball with city requirements enacted by voters, and almost overnight, the market was flooded with half a dozen companies that had a platform that was "good enough." Now that Uber has left the market, can they get back in? If they do, they're going to have to do something different to capture market share. I doubt that will come in the form of offering cheaper rides. In my opinion, it can only happen if Uber gets their act together about taking insights from their data. That is something that Uber does have over local rideshare companies: a vast pool of data to pull from. If they can figure out how to pull the correct data from that pool, I believe it is possible for them to offer a better customer, partner, and employee experience than any of their competitors in Austin. That is something that might make them attractive again.

Update: As this book went to print, the State of Texas voted to kill the city requirements that had pushed Uber out initially. Uber is now back! This has already begun to hurt other local rideshare operators that had come in to fill the void. In this case, consumers are more concerned with their need (a ride) rather than staying loyal to a brand. This is fortunate for Uber; Uber is superior in filling that need because of its hefty infrastructure and superior app. It seems to me that in this scenario, need trumps customer and employee care. It is now game over for the other, smaller operators.

GATHERING DATA CORRECTLY

How can we make sure that new and old companies alike turn out to be more like Facebook or Google and not like Uber in terms of utilizing data effectively?

Well, the good news is that we don't have to convince companies of the importance of understanding data; they already know just how important it is.

The problem is that a majority of incumbent companies, including some of the newer, fancy, millennial-led companies, think that they know how to use data and metrics to get insights into their customers or employees. They recognize the importance of collecting data from customers but can mistake what it all means. The data that they gather doesn't necessarily shed light on the customer experience in the way they think it does. They're fixated on looking at the data from various touch points but they're losing sight of the holistic journey—the lifecycle of the customer and the employees that serve them. They don't really understand who the customer is, because this means something different to every department, and so they are misinterpreting data and not understanding how to apply it appropriately.

They need to ask themselves if they are getting the most important data, what insights they are gaining from these metrics, and how they are applying the insights.

Let's dissect this issue with an example of a company that sells insurance.

A customer who is going through the process of purchasing insurance must interact with many different people in many different departments at the company. Every department in the company captures a couple of data points from the customer. However, none of them capture all points of data about the customer or integrate them into a cohesive picture of the customer. The salespeople might know that the customer is planning on purchasing another car and so must purchase more insurance. The invoicing people might know that the customer has paid his bill late every month. But neither knows about those data points that the other gathered.

Companies need to stop collecting data and insight in silos, and they need to start looking at it from a much broader context. Companies also need to realize that optimizing a single touch point in their data gathering efforts is not necessarily going to equal yield in terms of customer experience.

WHAT EMPLOYEE INSIGHTS LOOK LIKE AND WHERE TO FIND THEM

Companies are missing the boat entirely when it comes to understanding the importance of gathering data about employees. That is especially sad, because, as we've stated, many employees are the tip of the spear as they are the ones interacting with the customers. We want to make sure that all employees are happy and able to do their jobs... just like the employees at Google and Southwest Airlines.

How can we go about gathering employee insights so that we can make sure they are happy and able to perform their duties?

There is a lot of buzz about the "Net Promoter Score." Companies believe that the Net Promoter Score is the best indicator for how a customer feels about a company. Why isn't there an internal equivalent for employees? There really should be, because you can tell a lot about how a company is doing based on what their employees say about them. This has to go beyond an annual employee survey. Feedback needs to be continuous. I applaud David Skomo and the company he works at for being as serious as they are about employee engagement, and I believe they will only get better at it. Things take time.

Dawie has done something unprecedented: He has created a measurement tool that goes beyond any traditional measurement tool I have seen before. It is basically like a Net Promoter Score, because it measures shifts in employee sentiment across his org.

Plot twist: It really isn't a tool at all, it is just a simple question. He asks his employees, "What does a great day at work feel like for you?" (Dawie's team insists that the question actually came out as "What would it take for work not to suck?") The question evolved to include "What are the things that help me feel like I've had a great day?" and then, "How do I behave when I am living those things?"

Dawie came across the idea years ago when he was hired into a small bank that had gone through some significant upheavals that had broken the team. The CIO had left under bad terms, and it became clear that both he had been and many other members of the team now were in a significant amount of pain. They didn't feel trusted. They didn't feel valued. Some of them were even relegated to offices in the basement of the parking lot!

Dawie understood that in order to fix their piss-poor situation, he needed to "cut to the nub" of why everyone was so miserable, and make this go away. If they didn't feel good, it would be impossible for them to do good work. He had to meet their needs.

So he did. He realized that making that bank healthy had so little to do with fixing processes or introducing new technology. It was all about gathering employee insights to understand what their needs were, so that they could be happy and productive.

So he went around asking everyone what a great day for him or her would look like. Then, he worked to make it happen. How? The next step was to figure out how the current reality prevented them from experiencing that great day. Then, once they could see the roadblocks, they were given "permission" to try techniques that might move those roadblocks. Dawie says that they supported the "trying" part with "good coaches from a number of disciplines including Lean, Agile, and DevOps to ensure that people would be well equipped to try things intelligently."

It was wildly successful.

Dawie moved from that small bank to Standard Bank, where he saw more of the same thing: more people who were just plain miserable.

Dawie said that he always told himself that if he woke up enough mornings hating to go to work, then he would need to change jobs. But he knew that for many people, that freedom is a luxury. So, he continued to ask his one question, so no one would ever feel like their "job was a life sentence."

HOW TO GATHER EMPLOYEE INSIGHTS

Most companies use surveys to gather insights about the temperature of the org. That's it. Surveys are what these big, billion dollar conglomerates think are adequate thermometers to gauge the general internal temperature of the company.

A couple of yes/no questions. A couple of questions where you can choose 1, 2, 3, 4, or 5 stars. That's it.

Nothing else. That is how most companies determine if their employees are happy.

There are some companies out there that have begun to realize that this is no longer okay. I've seen them scramble to get something in the works. Unfortunately, they go grabbing surveys and buying expensive tools and other rather weak stuff like that. But before they start doing that, they need to know that there is a right way to gather data about their employees, and there is a wrong way.

Traditional surveys used in isolation are the wrong way. Surveys measure data about conformity to policy and procedure. Surveys are mainly for the benefit of the business, not for the employee.

What companies need to do is ask if their employees

are able to operate authentically in their jobs. Dawie's question prompts an answer that reveals authentic truth. Companies need to ensure, like Dawie does, that their employees can be their authentic selves. It is important, because when people aren't authentic, they will behave in a way that is not necessarily conducive to a good customer experience.

If a company wants to understand employee experience and gather employee insights from their call center folks, they should ask a couple of simple questions. They need to ask how employees are doing at their jobs. They need to ask how employees are performing work. Perhaps, after gathering answers, the company determines that their call center people go off script 90% of the time. The company then needs to determine why. Are the call center agents improperly trained, or does the script not make sense?

It is imperative to know, but so many companies don't know.

WHAT TO DO WITH EMPLOYEE INSIGHTS

Let's say that Joe is a salesman for his company, and he is pretty down because he can't get his job done correctly and so is unhappy and demotivated. Not only that, but his company doesn't collect insights about their employees, so Joe's anger goes unchecked. He feels like his only outlet is to talk poorly about the company on Facebook. Now Joe looks bad, and the company looks bad as well.

If that company had pursued insights about Joe and his coworkers, and shared them throughout the company, then things might have ended up differently.

Companies must allow for transparency and visibility. Once companies gather employee insights, it is crucial that they share them freely throughout the organization. Employees should have access to the data. Employees need to know what is happening so that they can participate in the conversation to affect a positive outcome for customers and employees.

Crowdsourcing would be a great addition to simply surveying employees. I'm a big believer in the efficacy of crowdsourcing. Crowdsourcing allows companies to find out who has the best idea, and who knows their stuff. It allows everyone to interact in a constructive nonconforming environment. In crowdsourcing environments, people feel safe to go ahead and throw their thoughts on the table. It is very pure-intentioned; employees are not trying to make waves or be critical of the company, they're just participating in a conversation.

If a company decides to try crowdsourcing, it needs to be wary of those few employees who will speak out not because they have a good idea or a particularly fierce passion for bettering the company, but because they want the attention. If leaders fall into the trap of these loudmouths, they might be too preoccupied with the false prophets and ignore the people who really do have the best solutions.

I've done a lot of projects over the past twenty years, and I've never seen a tool that can really separate out the noise, but Dawie found a way to separate the loud voices from the passionate voices.

Dawie said that he learned this lesson years ago, when he was a scuba instructor. He said that when you are first starting out, it is common to hold a free scuba course for friends and family to practice your teaching skills. Dawie found that when he held his course, very few people did the reading or even showed up. A wise old scuba instructor asked him how his course was going, and Dawie explained the situation. The scuba instructor told him that he knew why people weren't participating—it was because they "didn't value" what Dawie was giving them because he didn't make them work or pay for it. Basically, Dawie learned that people value things that are hard to get.

Dawie transferred this lesson to his employees. He went

to his employees and told them that he knew they weren't happy about things, and that he was offering seats at a table to fix them. The seat at the table was the vehicle for change, but only for those who truly wanted to help with change. They would have to earn their way to the table by passing a test in the form of a questionnaire.

He separated noise from passion through the results of a questionnaire that took him days to create. Separating out the noise wasn't as scientific as it sounded. In fact, it was simple. The questionnaire was designed to be a "pain in the ass" to complete. It was at least two hours long, and required employees to watch many videos and do a lot of reading. It prompted questions that were "not immediately apparent." Therefore, only the people who truly cared would work through the questionnaire.

The questionnaire was massively successful. The people who made it to the table through the quizzes did so because they badly wanted to help.

Few companies are there yet, but, man, they need to get there soon.

GETTING DATA WRONG

Companies are all about data, but they just haven't been able to get it right yet.

I caution companies to avoid being seduced by the shiny ball of technology when it comes to containing and collecting data. Purchasing every new tool means nothing in terms of success if those tools aren't utilized effectively toward desired outcomes and, especially, toward stronger customer and employee experiences.

Many companies are turning toward automation as a solution. There is a lot of value in automation, and there is also a lot of false value in automation. It is important to explore, though, because it is the future and has the potential to really impact employee and customer experience.

AUTOMATION

Automation helps companies get ahead of the curve because it allows them to integrate new technologies to optimize their businesses processes. In the beginning, automation was primarily seen as a way to reduce costs. That is still true to this day. However, more often, I see companies automate just to automate.

I understand why companies want everything to be automated. The competitive pressures out there require companies to be better, faster, and more agile. That is good, but they must understand that while automation is very helpful and beneficial in some cases, automating just for the sake of automating is not.

In their quest to get ahead with automation, companies forget just how delicate the relationship between humans and technology is. They lose sight of the potential impacts that it may have on the customer and the employee. They disproportionately emphasize the value of automation over the value of the employee, who in some ways, is already thought of as a machine themselves. There is nothing inherently bad about automation, but automating too much and too fast is, ultimately, a fool's game.

THE WRONG WAY TO AUTOMATE

Companies no longer want to just automate 20% of their back offices; they want to automate their whole back office—which means getting rid of their people. Companies need to stop thinking about eliminating employees from the equation, and start thinking about how they can strike an optimal balance between employees and machines. Automation shouldn't mean "taking humans out of the loop 100%." Remember, customers of every ilk prefer human interaction to digital channels when they have a problem to resolve. Artificial Intelligence is going to really come on to the scene in the coming years and will mimic human interaction. However, removing the human completely is just folly. We will always need empathy and creativity when engaging with each other in complex circumstances.

The balance should be looked at surgically. There should

be no broad-brush stroke application of automation. In my opinion, and from what I've seen, that optimal balance is struck when companies can provide their employees with machines that can automate busy-work for them, so that they can be freed up to do more important things. In the ideal world, employees would spend all of their newfound free time engaging with their customers.

Automation means that companies need employees more than ever. Humans deliver important value to back offices that machines simply can't deliver. That is because the world of customer engagement and customer experience necessitates human interaction.

AUTOMATION CASE STUDY

Right now, about 80% of our projects at BP3 since 2003 have dealt in some part with automation. In one particular case, some colleagues worked with an insurer to automate their mailroom.

The insurer got a lot of mail. Customers sent in payments or whole stacks of paperwork, and all of that funneled through—you guessed it—their mailroom. The folks in the mailroom had to take the mail, crack it open, read it, and determine what the hell department it belonged to. Then, they had to scan the papers and write up a synopsis about what that particular piece of mail was. Lastly, they delivered the mail to the appropriate department.

This whole process took a long time. Because the work was so tedious, it created a bottleneck effect, where mail would get stuck in processing in the mailroom. Employees were missing deadlines or were unable to stay on top of new information because their mail always came to them with significant lag.

The insurer had had enough, so everyone sat down to brainstorm how to fix the slow mailroom. The problem was, every single step of the process was necessary, so they couldn't eliminate a single step. It was ultimately decided that the insurer's mailroom was a perfect environment to integrate automation.

One of the biggest factors that contributed to the lagging mail was the fact that each piece of mail had to be analyzed and sorted based on what department it needed to go to. So they injected OCR, a character recognition process where a scanning system could pick up or "read" up to 90% of correspondence. It could determine the content of that piece of mail and from there, it sorted it based on what department the content correlated to. They also automated the scanning portion of the process, which sped up the cycle as well.

The new system was able to get information out faster and mail in the hands of the employees more efficiently. But most importantly, it prevented the insurer from having to pay people to sit in a mailroom, ripping open envelopes. Instead, those people could focus on more profound and important things, such as improving quality control.

The project was a success. For example, if Wal-Mart, an insured customer, had sent in a ledger to change their amount of insured employees from 3,000 to 5,000 for that billing period, it might have gotten stuck in the mailroom, and the employees in billing might have missed the memo. This might have had a cascading effect, where the insurer sent out the bill for 3,000 employees, and Wal-Mart would have gotten pissed because they had sent in a message telling the insurance company that they needed to cover 5,000. Who gets in trouble? The guys in billing get in trouble for sending out the wrong invoice. But it's not their fault; the letter was stuck in the mailroom getting processed.

The work that takes place in the mailroom is pretty low value, but it impacts the business and profoundly impacts the customer.

So my client automated all that mess. Every bit of it. They input some intelligence into the system and, boom! Mail on the appropriate desk within hours.

AUTOMATION LEADS TO HIGHER-VALUE INTERACTIONS

Automation is more than just cost reduction and time optimization. It is about freeing the employee to have higher fidelity interactions. The work that employees need to be doing now is a much higher-valued kind of work than before, but employees don't have the time to do that because they are bogged down with trivial duties. Through automation, employees can factor in the luxury of time as a function of their work, and leverage that time into getting better insight into what that customer journey really is.

There are a lot of wasteful work operations that automation can eliminate for employees. Often, I see an employee sitting at their computer with seven different applications open, trying desperately to find and understand a problem or fulfill a request. These seven different applications have to be used in various ways for various tasks, and none of them really paints a good picture for the employee. He might have to swivel across consoles for hours when he could be spending that time talking with his customer. Typically, in a scenario like that, I will hear the customer service representative tell the customer that he needs to put her on hold. The customer will have to sit there listening to music, sometimes for a very long time, while the customer service rep frantically parses through information so that he can assist her. He isn't doing rocket science; he is literally just trying to get into other applications and retrieve data and pull together the story of the customer.

But what if he had a tool or machine that could do all of that busy-work for him? That is why RPA (which I mentioned previously) is becoming more popular. The robotic software systems sit on employees' desktops and can do all of that tedious searching for the customer service rep. Better yet, that RPA can search at the speed of a computer, so our customer doesn't have to be put on hold, and our customer service rep can get back to the most important part: the customer.

A lot of companies are getting to the point where they see their employees having to perform very low value tasks and getting paid too much money to do this. RPA solves that problem, because it takes over the mundane work that human capital does not need to be wasted on. It is an example of smart automation.

These interactions will allow a higher intimacy level, which is more important than ever because we live in a world where quality of experience and delighting the customer with every touch matter as much or more than factors like cost and speed.

I can only imagine what this relationship will look like

when artificial intelligence (AI) really comes in and takes over the human intelligence aspect of that partnership. I believe that we are a few years off from that. But the notion of AI is a cool thing to think about, and it is very real.

At BP3, we built an AI prototype that dealt with customer disputes. We used some technology from IBM: a baby version of Watson. We fed it patterns, including sentiment, and told it what those patterns meant. It takes a good chunk of time to get that system and all other AI systems learning and doing what they should be doing properly. As I mentioned earlier, AI will get better, surely, but it will be years and years before it is mainstream. There are a lot of things that must be considered, such as cost effectiveness. When that happens, ideally, AI will work alongside—and not instead of—humans.

But right now, there are bigger problems that need to be dealt with in the short run. In my mind, a bigger problem is how to capture and action all of the insights that data and automation allows us to capture.

INTEGRATED PERSPECTIVES

In the short run, companies need to provide platforms that bring together all of the different data and insights that float around in an organization. This will enable all within the company to have an integrated perspective, aka, a shared view, about what is going on and what needs to be done.

I worked with a private mortgage insurer out of the Bay Area. After the housing collapse in 2008, they realized that they had lost their integrated perspective and needed help getting their world back together. Of course, they only realized this once their world was on fire, so, they more or less had no choice in the matter. They were bleeding out, and their industry had crumbled, and it wasn't until

2012 that they really got their asses into high gear. It was too late, but honestly, *better late than never*. They learned a lot about themselves, I have no doubt.

They got all hands on deck. They assessed what they were doing wrong. They realized that the company was comprised of silos that were all working toward their own individual goals. Everyone was pulling resources for themselves and hoarding their time. The leaders of the company realized they couldn't operate in silos anymore.

All of the employees came together and sat in a room and figured out what the biggest problems for the company as a whole were and what the best solutions to fix those problems were. They set a strict goal that no one was allowed to interpret. Ultimately, their goal was to create a mortgage insurance origination system.

They went around the company and looked at all of the projects that were going on. If a project didn't directly support the goal, then it was cut off. They cleared out all of the crap. They restricted all financial flows into only the crucial places.

It took them a while to streamline the process. It was clunky at first, because no one had ever had to do it before, but they worked through it.

It was a terrible time for them, but once they integrated perspectives, the business actually picked up speed. They were able to accelerate ideas and solutions faster. They had clarity into what needed to happen and where support needed to go. There were no project collisions, where everyone was fighting for power, people, and resources. It was fantastic. Everyone had a shared vision. Integrating perspectives had an extremely powerful impact.

This company pivoted faster than I've ever seen any company pivot. But they had to; things were going sideways, and the ship was sinking.

INTEGRATING PERSPECTIVES AT WESTPAC

Dawie knew the value of integrating perspectives despite the fact that his company was still printing money, and despite the fact that their world was not on fire.

Diverging perspectives happen, primarily, as a result of silos. Unfortunately, it is very easy to accidentally create silos because, as Dawie puts it, when you strategize and then bring that strategy to life, you naturally move toward taking capabilities and making boxes out of them, which results in discrete organizational units. Then, you take those units and figure out how to manage them and make them effective and efficient, and take as much risk as possible out of them. Then, you put people into those boxes to fulfill those particular descriptions. Then, you work to figure out how to incentivize those people to manage resources. Then, inevitably, a couple of years down the line, you come back and say, "Oh shit! We just completely screwed up our culture by creating silos and everyone hates us." This was the path of least intellectual commitment because those steps are pretty easy and logical to follow.

Silos happen. We accidentally created them at BP3. They can happen to any business, regardless of size and leaders' best intentions.

So how do we prevent siloing and ensure integrated perspectives? Dawie outlined an exercise that he has used a couple of times within his own organizations and with a number of MBA cohorts to prevent siloing and promote integrated perspectives.

First, he said, you must create a grand vision. You need that vision because you have to remind everyone of the fight that you are fighting.

A great example of a vision is one where you put the customer first in everything that you work toward: "When you examine what it means to put the customer first in everything you do, there are some particular capabilities that you need to have to be able to do that. You need to have the capability of actually engaging directly with actual customers." You must be able to have great conversations with them. You must put those customers and those conversations at the forefront of your mind. If everyone is thinking that way, you will be unified in your strategy no matter what part you play in it. Silos will not be able to afford having biases.

If you have a greater vision and communicate it frequently, people will work together collaboratively rather than simply according to like capabilities. As Dawie put it, when people are grouped by like capability, it is "100% destructive." When you manage people scientifically—in the production-line style or the waterfall style, where everyone is grouped by like capability—no one is part of the greater vision. Your employees will begin to feel like they are only a piece in the "mechanical box" they've been put in.

Putting people into a box makes them unhappy. They want to work in a team, to be a part of the greater outcome. They want to work for the bigger vision of the company.

Dawie found a way to integrate his employees' perspectives by eliminating silos. I wondered what an organization without traditional siloed functional units looked like, so I asked him what changes he made to how his organization was structured.

He told me that he couldn't inflict a formal change model on his people. They would have rejected him. Instead, he found that you must allow people to change the organization to best fit their needs. The new structure will come organically.

People will figure out the difference between operating models and organization structures. An operating model is how things are done, and the org structure is how people are tied together. When change happens organically, the org structure stops being something that sits on top of people and becomes something that sits alongside people. This inherently eliminates the line bosses or managers who sit over people. Instead, the people traditionally known as "managers" become custodians of a technical discipline. The "manager" doesn't own the outcome; rather, the entire team owns it.

Once you allow organic change, you will start to hear people talk about the deficiencies of the old org. Leaders need to develop finely tuned ears to start hearing those keywords to figure out how to source a new organizational structure. Dawie said, "Invariably an organizational structure that is sourced in this way will be much, much simpler than the one we would've created the other way around, mainly because there's so much less need for command and control, and so much more need for coaching, facilitation, skill development, and support. The entire org structure basically becomes an enabling structure as opposed to a command and control structure."

Once you can do this, you can reorg the whole organization. This requires a fair amount of faith and a whole bunch of patience from leaders. But once the seeds are sown, the return is exponential. It becomes viral quickly, and people will adopt that positive mindset all on their own.

Once the organization can restructure itself organically, the definition of "leadership" will change. Leaders will no longer *lead* processes. They will begin to, as Dawie put it, "make the processes possible." Instead of telling their employees what to do, leaders will realize that their job is "not to be at the front of the army on [their] white horses swinging [their] large swords. [Their] job will be to sit at the back of the army, making sure that all of the troops know how to swing their swords and are the very best swordsmen that they could be."

Leaders will begin to let their employees figure out what works best for them. Dawie learned that, quite predictably, when people are allowed to decide how they want to work, they move toward Lean and Agile philosophies.

Dawie told me that he and his team began implementing changes at Westpac in August of 2015. In eighteen months, the team crowdsourced their new organizational structure, and the metrics have been off the charts. Their efficiencies are three to four times what they were before they began.

The cool part is that Dawie told me that they were about to dismantle the organization again, and make a new iteration based on improvements that everyone feels are essential.

This process allowed Dawie to ultimately integrate perspectives and get all of his employees happy, on the same page, and working toward the ultimate goal: a happy customer.

INTEGRATING IS HARD

Dawie makes it sound easy, but in reality, integrating perspectives is difficult to do. When we talk about integrated perspectives, we mostly mean the "perspective" that employees have in regard to the customer. What does the customer want? What does the customer need? How do we care for the customer? We must recognize that everyone within a company has a different perspective when it comes to these questions.

Each employee has his or her own bias. For example, let's say that Customer X has had continual difficulty implementing a specific software solution. Salespeople might see that problem and try to sell the customer consulting services to help them implement the software. The account management team might see it as a problem with an uneducated implementation specialist. Account management might just suggest giving those implementation specialists a guided tutorial. Perhaps the IT people see the fact that Customer X is unable to implement the software as a technical issue. IT might want to go to the customer's office to check to make sure that they can integrate the software with their preexisting systems. Regardless of what the solution should be, all of these teams have different perspectives on how to deal with Customer X's problem.

It would be bad if all three teams were trying to talk to Customer X to tell them what to do. There would be too much noise, and Customer X might get pissed. What sales, account management, and IT need to do before they approach Customer X is sit down and figure out a single way to tackle the problem. In order to do this effectively, they need to integrate their perspectives about what is going wrong with Customer X.

For that reason, it is important that companies have a way for their various teams to integrate their perspectives. This solution should come in the form of a platform that allows employees to integrate perspectives and insights in order to fix problems and achieve goals.

This will allow the salespeople, account management team, IT folks, and anyone else who is involved to offer the absolute best customer experience for Customer X and all of the company's other customers.

HOW HARD IS IT?

So few companies can integrate perspectives.

So many companies make the mistake of doing this piecemeal and myopically. I have seen companies relying on the perspective of one or two functional groups within the organization. Sometimes, companies rely more heavily on the perspectives of the salespeople because they drive revenue, and ignore the perspectives of the people in IT. Other companies only really care about what those at the very top think, because they are the "leaders" and ignore those at the bottom who deal directly with the customer. They rarely take into consideration the opinions and perspectives of the other groups.

Then, those companies wonder why they don't get the yield they are looking for. They haven't done the necessary integration of perspectives! They don't really understand the whole picture! Without this whole picture—without seeing or understanding the whole puzzle—companies really don't know what it is that they should be doing.

HOW CAN COMPANIES INTEGRATE PERSPECTIVES?

Companies must first understand the importance of listening to all functional departments within the company. Every single touch point (person or department) in the customer experience should be included in the conversation. The employee experience and their insights all need to be integrated. Silos need to come down because the customer experience cuts across those silos, and it is only when the silos come down that anyone can get a holistic view of those perspectives. Everyone needs to be able to be a part of the conversation and log all of their insights and data points into a platform. In this case, the sum of the parts does not equal the whole.

Companies need to provide an adequate platform where employees can voice their perspectives. Currently, most companies offer tooling that is insufficient. It is insufficient primarily because it is usually applicable to only one group. I'm talking about platforms like SalesForce and Marketta that offer communication platforms for sales and marketing, respectively. However, there are a couple platforms designed for enterprise-wide leadership management that should be examined. One that comes to mind is Khorus. I have had great experiences using Khorus. Khorus aligns the strategy and goals of an organization from the individual contributor all the way up, down, and sideways from the CEO. Interestingly enough, it was designed by Joel Trammell, a successful CEO who experienced the gap of organizational alignment firsthand. Joel is a long-time entrepreneur and investor in the Austin technology scene who wrote a book called *The CEO Tightrope*, which I recommend reading!

In order to properly integrate perspectives, companies need to implement a holistic platform where everyone can input data and take away insights. It's important for companies to have a platform for integrating all their perspectives and insights in order to achieve the goals, initiatives, and—the brass ring that everyone's after—customer experience.

THE PLUMBING

The "platform" that I speak of should not be a one-and-done solution implemented in a single area. Rather, it should be thought of as "plumbing." Like the plumbing in a house, this "plumbing" needs to bind together processes and act as a channel that connects all of the "rooms" or departments in a company. The plumbing in a company should connect the people, processes, and technology within it. By doing that, the plumbing acts as a platform where everyone can integrate his or her perspectives.

Proper plumbing allows companies to work toward digital transformation. Plumbing is where digital platforms can bring the reality of those integrated perspectives and processes into play. Melding a digital operations platform with the digital front-end is where the juice is: You get the whole journey of the customer and the employee.

Plumbing is important because it allows companies to deal effectively with the processes that cut across organizations. The plumbing is what allows integrated perspectives to travel throughout a company in a unified way, so there is no waste in the system and all of the employees can understand the holistic needs of the customer.

Historically, this plumbing has not incorporated business process management platforms and decision systems, which, if harmonized correctly, have a ton of real value. Instead, the plumbing has primarily been ad hoc.

Companies need better plumbing than they've traditionally had. They need plumbing that takes in data across an organization, makes it readable by everyone, and allows insights to be taken out of it. In order to make all of this data clear and easily digestible to employees, customers, and third parties alike, companies need a viable orchestration and instrumentation process platform. By "viable," I mean that this platform will need to perform a couple of important duties. It will need to be able to gather and consume information that comes from many different channels. It will also need to assess and log customer needs and desires in real time. It will have to provide companies with appropriate data so they can operate proactively rather than reactively when it comes to customer interactions. It should enhance the customer journey by aiding the employee journey. Ultimately, a viable platform will act as a vehicle for companies to have an integrated perspective about how employee experience and engagement correlates with customer experience and engagement.

Although I am beginning to see more kinds of programs and projects that are about using processes as a platform for digital transformation, I don't think anyone is really there yet. If companies were creating effective plumbing, customer service would be getting better, not worse.

Trustmark, a bank holding company, revamped their process plumbing. They reinvented a part of their go-to-market strategy for their loan origination process. They made the strategy more robust and brought in third parties to help them automate, so they can gather data more quickly. They are also taking steps to collect insights on their employees to determine where employees are spending the most time, and where the bottlenecks are. They are looking at how employees are interacting with their systems and gathering insights on customers.

Trustmark is doing better than most companies. Trustmark realized that in order to improve, they needed to get past the idea that process implementation is only necessary in one or two areas. Instead, they understood that building adequate plumbing is a never-ending battle that must take place across all sections of the organization. It needs to be omnipresent so that it can cast a wide net and go deep.

Plumbing must cast a wide net because that affords the company a unified view of the customer. The net pulls in information about the customer in real time. It should collect all the customer data in one fell swoop (profile, stats, credit rating, geography, etc.). All of this information needs to be available on demand and easily accessible by all so that everyone is on the same page.

Some companies get to the point where the net is cast wide enough, but they still fail because they don't maintain the net. They think that as long as that net is thrown out there, that is all that is needed. They don't realize that they have to continually cast out, monitor, and care for the net. Employees are busy; they are under a lot of pressure and have a million things to do, and the cadence of business moves faster every day. I've been in meetings with countless employees from countless organizations. They are generally tired. Some look like they have had the shit kicked out of them. But it is crucial that they summon the energy to cast this net time and time again in order to have a holistic view of processes and customer health. They need to be reminded that casting the net is imperative.

Most of the time, there is no mandate from above to fix the plumbing. On a couple of occasions, when my team and I get started on a new project, the employees will come to us and tell us that they've been told by their managers that they really aren't allowed to help us with our initiatives.

We've met a lot of resistance when trying to get projects going and the plumbing working. We've had to deal with reluctant managers who don't talk to anyone else in any other departments. We've had cases where employees in one department have told us that they aren't allowed to talk to employees in other departments. Other times, we've had employees say that they can dedicate only 20% of their time to us because they have four other projects to work on in addition to their day job. In some organizations, there is so much pressure coming from all directions that they've snapped. Even when the leadership says, "Gosh dang it, we all really need to get on the same page here, and get the plumbing working," they can't. Their organizations are already crumbling beneath them.

TOOLING FOR CHANGE

Oftentimes, companies are unable to initiate the placement of proper plumbing because they don't have the proper tooling to do so. By "tooling," I mean both technical and non-technical instruments that help companies operate optimally.

There is a lot of tooling out there that is viable and often even affordable, relatively speaking. But most of the time, tooling either doesn't get used, or isn't used in the most effective way. If tooling is used effectively, it can really make significant changes and deliver value to a company. Unfortunately, most companies don't understand most of the abilities of their tooling, and they readily overproduce requirements. Most companies still use Excel spreadsheets and email to pass along data and messages. Those companies are stuck in the past.

Some companies think that they need to throw a lot of money at the problem in order to get the "best" tooling. Much of the time, those companies end up paying for expensive custom platforms. The problem, though, is that custom solutions are often not the best solution for a company. Custom platforms are not always suited for rapid change, so they prevent a company from staying agile and amenable to change. Other times, custom solutions don't integrate well with preexisting digital ecosystems. Companies end up creating a walled garden with their custom systems. I often see custom solutions that don't actually solve problems for a company because they either weren't designed using the appropriate data, or were designed for a perceived problem that occurred years ago.

Sometimes, companies flounder not because of their deficient technical tooling, but because of their insufficient non-technical tooling. Non-technical tooling is also known as "methodology." Often, companies need to improve their methods in order to create better plumbing. For instance, let's say a company is having problems because various functional groups are having difficulty communicating. Maybe the solution for that company is not to build some custom-messaging app, but rather to just literally yell at Jerry down the hall to "Stop doing that!" or "Send that report off immediately!" Let's be honest: Jerry isn't going to be checking that fancy app. He can barely work his flip phone. (Yes, there are still many Jerry's out there.) Sometimes, you really don't have to invest in technology to do simple things. Technology is an enabling function, not a silver bullet. A lot of times, you just need to get scrappy.

Sometimes it's more about changing the culture of your company. It is less about getting the best tooling and more about giving your employees the authority to act. Or, it is about crowdsourcing and giving your employees a voice. Occasionally, the most powerful and meaningful changes require little to no technology. Technology and platforms and decent plumbing is all good and well, but they aren't the end all, end all.

When Dawie was changing things up at Westpac, he did not focus on buying new tooling in order to enact change. Rather, he used cultural and humanistic approaches in establishing and strengthening the plumbing. He found that ceremonies were massively impactful. He says that he is "fanatical" about instituting ceremonies in regular life at companies, because this is a great channel by which to strengthen communication. He schedules regular showcases and open mic style meetings where anyone can talk about what they did, what they learned, or what they need help with. He also instituted "culture champions" who are "custodians of the process by which we check in to make sure that people are okay."

By widening communication channels, Dawie allowed disgruntled and worried employees to have a voice and state their opinions openly. Employees used those sessions to talk about how they would like the plumbing to work. Then, the participants were tasked with taking their ideas back to the rest of their colleagues and testing them to see what those colleagues' reactions were. Dawie wanted to make sure that everyone was included so that nobody felt like things were being "inflicted" upon them. He wanted to ensure every team was represented in every session.

Sometimes, as in Dawie's case, the Lean-Agile method is the best-recommended route for implementing successful plumbing. Lean-Agile incorporates Agile technologies such as Agile software development techniques like DevOps that have Lean concepts built into their processes. But basically, it isn't a technical system. It is literally just asking the question, "How do we take waste out of our world?"

There are so many things that companies do that are just so wasteful. The Lean-Agile method is all about eliminating waste from everything from project implementation to the business processes themselves, to the platform and departments. It can help to remove overproduction, down time, and shipping inefficiencies. It can get rid of the unnecessary policy and compliance stuff that people are told they have to do.

You can determine what "waste" is by conducting a value stream analysis on the processes. You ask yourself what gives customers value (value add), what adds no value (non-value), what is a required non-value add (things you have to do because of risk or compliance), and what takes value away. Eighty-five percent of the process is usually non-value add, and only 15% adds value. There is absolutely a shit ton of waste everywhere.

Using Agile methods, you work to eliminate things that

take value away from customers and/or don't add any value to their experience. Lean-Agile based methods are used in software development, but are also applicable to non-technical endeavors across functional departments including, but not limited to, sales, account management, and marketing.

ROOT CAUSE

At its core, fixing and laying down good plumbing is just about understanding "root-cause analysis" to come up with the best solutions. When companies look at problems, they only really look at, understand, and ultimately try to solve the symptoms of their problems. But they really need to look for the root cause of their problems and attack that.

Let's analyze an overly simplified example. Let's look at the problem of misbilling. Sometimes, a company will generate miscalculated invoices month after month. Customers get pissed; that is the effect of the misbilling. Companies work through this problem by apologizing to the customer. They work to amend their mistakes by sending out a new invoice and spending more time making sure their customer feels loved.

But what they actually need to do is dive deep into the causal side. Employees don't move along the chain to see exactly where the problem of misbilling stems from. They are only focused on retroactively solving misbilling. They don't work to fix it proactively. If they move along the chain far enough, they might realize (and this is usually the case) that there are multiple contributing causes to the problem. Then there is the root cause. But they can only find that root cause once they analyze all of the secondary and tertiary causes.

Once they can fix that root problem, guess what? No more misbilling! Problem solved.

Normally, it doesn't take a ton of work to figure out the root problem, quantify it, and prove that it is real. But again, the hardest part is having to work across siloed departments.

A real world example comes from Transportation, a large moving company that relocates giant companies across the country. When the company's salespeople are selling their services, they pretty much tell potential clients whatever they want to hear. The guys over in sales sell the product whichever way it is asked for without really making sure that the request is possible to fulfill. They end up selling exotic shit, such as patterns and configurations that might not be possible or available. If the potential client wants to be billed every third Friday of the month, and their bill needs to be on pink paper, and the courier that delivers it needs to tap dance and sing, Transportation's salespeople will tell potential customers that they can offer that.

But then, when the request for a singing courier hits fulfillment and logistics, Transportation tell the client, no, we cannot fulfill that request. The sales guys promised the customer something that the business can't fulfill, perhaps because it conflicts with a strict anti-singing courier policy at the company. Now, there is conflict because the company's salespeople made promises. The folks at fulfillment whip out the velvet hammer because they have to tell the salespeople that they have to go back to their potential client and tell them, no, they can't offer a tap dancing, singing courier.

So, here we have a problem. What is the root cause? One potential cause might be the fact that the salespeople pretty much offer anything that they feel will land them the deal. Yes, that is a legitimate problem, but not the root problem in this scenario.

The root cause is that there is some constraint somewhere that prohibits fulfillment from sending out a tap dancing courier. No one can really say *why* he or she can't send out a tap dancing courier, *it's just always been done a certain way.*

That constraint is potentially a required non-value add.

It is wasteful and unnecessary and causes problems both for the employees and the customers. That dumb stuff is stopping the sale from happening. What is the solution? Eliminate the wasteful rule that helps no one and hurts everyone. If we go ahead and attack the root cause, the effects go away. All the failure modes and the cascading effect that the failure modes have will instantly disappear.

CHANGE NOW

Customers don't care about the inside baseball of processes behind the scenes at a company. They want their product. They want the outcome that they were promised. They want you to make it work, make it fit, make it happen. By hook or by crook. They don't give a damn. Customers don't care about how the sausage is made, they just want to eat it.

If they aren't given what they purchased or what they were promised, they leave and go to any one of your competitors down the road.

We live in an era of great disruption. Technology and ethos have allowed many players to enter industry space and compete with the big incumbents. Customers have choices. Are they going to choose the agile, customer-focused, streamlined business? Or are they going to stick with their clunky, slow, and bottom line-focused incumbents?

You bet your ass they are going to the former. That is, unless those companies in the latter category can change.

They must pivot to prioritize offering fantastic employee engagement and external customer engagement, in addition to fixing or implementing excellent plumbing.

Change of that magnitude is hard, and the fact is that a lot of companies can't do it because they continue to try to institute change from the top. The actions of change must be made from the bottom up. The leadership has to provide a vehicle that facilitates change, the focus on a strategic intent. They have to provide an atmosphere where employees feel free to experiment. But that is really all that the top needs to do. Their job isn't to *tell* everyone how things need to be, their job is to have a vision and then allow the employees the freedom to find out the best way to accommodate it from an integrated perspective. That is how change really happens.

Dawie approached change in this exact fashion. Dawie provided the canvas and brushes, and told his employees to knock themselves out. He asked them to tell *him* how things needed to work. He told them to leave no stone unturned, to crowdsource ideas, to talk among themselves, and to organize themselves the way they needed to in order to do their jobs.

This provided change at a rapid pace. The other way, the top down, sort of approach? Yeah, that doesn't work.

These changes are all within reach; it is just a matter of will.

CONCLUSION

A MATTER OF WILL

Change is all just a matter of will—100% of the time.

There is nothing holding back a company from changing. There are no constraints on will. There are no constraints that should prevent a company from focusing on their employees and customers. There are no monetary constraints. There are no tooling or technological constraints. There are no regulatory or compliance constraints. There is no valid reason for a company to blame inaction on "constraints." They can't blame the government, regulation, policy, conformity, or command and control. Constraints can be overcome.

There are no constraints on will other than people's own applied myths and perceived limitations.

They just have to get on with it by believing with all that is holy that change is the right thing to do.

There is nothing standing between a company and its first steps toward change. It just takes *leadership* dropping the hammer and saying that *we are going to change*.

We are now going to focus on employee experience. We are now going to focus on customer experience. We are now going to create better plumbing through new platforms. We are now going to make employees feel safe by showing them that their leaders are human also. We are going to give them authority to act and also allow them to fail. We are going to educate, communicate frequently, allow constructive nonconformity, and integrate our perspectives.

It is hard. I'm not saying that it isn't. None of this is simple shit. It will be hard. But the rewards are worth it.

If companies can turn their ships around, it will change the world. This is not bullshit. It is not Silicon Valley spin. If companies can change, they will literally change the world.

We need them to. This kind of change is the harbinger of tremendous innovation.

In the TV series *The Newsroom*, there was a particular

episode where one of the characters was being interviewed in an auditorium filled with college students. One
of the students asked him what he thought it was that
made America the greatest country in the world.

"It's not the greatest country in the world," he said. "That's
my answer. And with a straight face, you're gonna tell students that America is so star-spangled awesome that we're
the only ones in the world who have freedom? Canada
has freedom. Japan has freedom. The UK, France, Italy,
Germany, Spain, Australia, and Belgium have freedom!
Of 207 sovereign states in the world, like 180 of them have
freedom. There's absolutely no evidence to support the
statement that we're the greatest country in the world.
We're 7th in literacy, 27th in math, 22nd in science, 49th
in life expectancy, 178th in infant mortality, 3rd in median
household income, 4th in labor force and 4th in exports.
We lead the world in only three categories: number of
incarcerated citizens per capita, number of adults who
believe angels are real, and defense spending, where we
spend more than the next twenty-six countries combined,
twenty-five of whom are allies."

America used to be great. We built incredible technologies.
We cured diseases. We put men on the moon. There was
a passion for exploring and trying things, but all of that is
gone now. What we have left is what we have left.

We're at the brink of a revolution. I know it sounds cheesy, but I'm not kidding here.

PEOPLE DRIVEN REVOLUTION

The revolution is being driven by people—employees and customers alike.

Peoples' attitudes have changed, and companies are failing to keep up.

There is a whole generation that's coming into the workforce who won't *perhaps* but rather *will* take pitchforks and torches and burn the fucking joint down as the status quo persists. That is the future of the workforce. It's already beginning. No longer will this young workforce simply conform to incongruent policies and procedures of corporations that have no analog in their own life experiences.

Yet businesses are still trying to enforce conformity in the workplace and subdue authenticity. Companies know that the more conforming something is, the more standardized it is, the more stable it is, and the less risk it will bring. Companies want to maintain stability, so they gravitate toward conformity. But they can no longer do that because Millennials demand authenticity, which undermines conformity. The pressure is being applied to companies to change, and rightly so.

If companies continue to refuse to change, I foresee a mutiny. In the not too distant future, our entitlement-minded Millennials will all have their own brand, their own profile, their own network, their own expertise, and their own value, and they won't need the brand of a corporation. They'll be supported by others in their peer group. Companies will begin to lose out on the best and brightest. To prevent this, companies must quickly organize themselves in a way that will empower people, give them permission to act, and allow employees to be themselves.

Dawie understood the revolution. But most leaders at companies all over the world do not. Nor do those leaders care; they are in an economic upswing, and they're printing money. Nothing is on fire for them. Nothing at Westpac was on fire either, but Dawie saw around corners and realized that, soon, it might be.

He took his leadership skills and willed the company to change. Dawie was the right leader for the time. He knew that this change was about people—customers and employees alike.

He understood the impact employee experience has on revenue, profit, and competition.

He knew he had to take care of his employees, and that

he could do it by asking one question: "What does a great day at work look like for you?" It was an honest and self-reflective question, and one that very few leaders will ever ask. There is often too much bias, too much self-serving ambition, and too much motivated skepticism and cynicism to seek the truth.

Not seeking the truth is the virus of all viruses, and will no doubt be any company's undoing. A virus can stay dormant in the body for a long period of time, and you will never know you have it until that moment that pressure is applied. The virus will get exposed, and then it will cascade and be relentless in its undoing.

If a company can transform correctly and rid themselves of the virus, it will put them on the moon. They will be able to do incredibly powerful things.

Sometimes, when I start a new project and I meet the employees, I feel sorry for them. Their burden is the elephant in the room; everyone knows it, but no one speaks about it.

They spend a third of their life in an environment that makes them feel powerless. It's fucking incredible how stress impacts your body, your home life, your happiness, and the happiness of others around you.

I absolutely feel for those employees. I empathize, I know what they're going through. I've been there, and I've seen it countless times in countless organizations. I've seen the same face, the same eyes, the same look, the same posture, and the same crick in the neck. I've seen the despondency, the lack of joy, and the fear.

I want to help companies help their employees. Most people want to do the best job that they can, and they want to bring joy to other's lives. There is no reason why companies shouldn't encourage those employees to reach their full potential.

Since the employee experience is directly correlated to the customer experience, if companies elevate the employee, the customer will benefit as well. That is a fact. You can sit at your desk all day long thinking about how to improve your customers' experience through mobile apps or shiny new products, but the only thing that will make a difference is if you lift up your employees. The happier your employees are, the happier your customers will be.

The employee experience is the alpha and omega of your destiny. It is the omniscient, omnipresent entity that rules the company. If you focus on the employee, everything else will happen for you.

DO IT NOW

I understand and am very sympathetic to the fact that change takes time; it is not an overnight thing. If a company starts today with the best intentions, it will to take them a good bit of time to get where they need to be. One of Dawie's iterations took about eighteen months to accomplish, and he's a seasoned pro.

Companies can do it if they have the right leader(s) to lead the way. The right leader will have the guts to affect change. The right leader will know that change cannot be done *to* an organization. Leaders can't force things; they can only clear a path and then empower their employees to not be conformists, and give them authorization to act. The employees will take care of the rest. The right leader has to amass an army with a singular vision, an integrated perspective, and authenticity. If a CEO tries to turn the rudder all by himself from a top down standpoint, his rudder might be an inch long. But if his employees are happy, they will be happy to help him and will rally behind him in turning the ship. He will find that, suddenly, the rudder is fifty feet long. The ship will turn.

Dawie has personally led change within a company three times. He is no one trick pony. What he has done is unprecedented. I have never seen another company with the lifespan of Westpac do what he enabled it to do. I've seen many people attempting the journey but failing because of biases and myth and antiquated bullshit silos that are no longer relevant. Dawie's opinion is shaped by reality. If I'm going to gamble, I'm taking Dawie with me.

Like I said before, I did things wrong in the beginning. I did them wrong for a long time. I got caught flat-footed. Mistakes happen. BP3 was growing fast—45% to 50% year over year—and we started allocating people, based on capabilities, into functional groups. It happened so subtly and quietly. There were no immediate shrieks of pain.

Creating organizational monsters is very easy to do. It's the way things have always been done, and it is very hard to untrain people. We recognized that we had done it ourselves, when we took an honest assessment, we realized that in two years, our wheels could come off. We understood the consequences, so we changed. We did it for our employees and our customers.

Companies must be aware, though, that hiring someone like us or poaching someone like Dawie won't necessarily get them that change they desire. We can educate them, show them, and tell them. But we can't *do it* for them. We can show them the way. We can show them the art of the possible. We can show them how things will hang together, what the plumbing will look like, and what will happen to them. But we can't do it for them.

This is the wake up call. If companies ignore the coming revolution, they will cease to exist. But, if they wake up and embrace it, then they will help change the world for the better and innovation and productivity will skyrocket in every industry. Everyone will win: employees, customers, business leaders, and the organization itself.

They just need the will to do it. Once they can get the will, there is absolutely nothing—I mean *nothing*—that can stop them. It worked for Dawie and for myself, and it works for others.

It will work for you.

It will work for anyone.

It will work in any industry.

You just have to will it.

ABOUT THE AUTHOR

 **LANCE GIBBS** is the Founder and Executive Chairman of BP3, a multi-award-winning organization that works with clients to accelerate, innovate, and simplify their process solutions. He is a Certified Master Black Belt in Six Sigma and an OCEB-Advanced BPM Expert with twenty years of experience helping top companies across many industries manage and transform their internal workings. Lance lives in Austin, Texas, with his incredible wife, Dana, and their three kick-ass kids, Kegan, Gia, and Alexa.